JIM
ABBOTT

GREAT ACHIEVERS

LIVES OF THE PHYSICALLY CHALLENGED

JIM ABBOTT

MAJOR LEAGUE PITCHER

NORMAN L. MACHT

Chelsea House Publishers

New York • Philadelphia

CHELSEA HOUSE PUBLISHERS

EDITORIAL DIRECTOR   Richard Rennert
EXECUTIVE MANAGING EDITOR   Karyn Gullen Browne
COPY CHIEF   Robin James
PICTURE EDITOR   Adrian G. Allen
ART DIRECTOR   Robert Mitchell
MANUFACTURING DIRECTOR   Gerald Levine

GREAT ACHIEVERS: LIVES OF THE PHYSICALLY CHALLENGED

SENIOR EDITOR   Kathy Kuhtz Campbell
SERIES DESIGN   Basia Niemczyc

Staff for **JIM ABBOTT**
EDITORIAL ASSISTANT   Kelsey Goss
PICTURE RESEARCHER   Sandy Jones
DESIGN ASSISTANT   Catherine Ho
COVER ILLUSTRATION   Daniel O'Leary

First Printing

1   3   5   7   9   8   6   4   2

Library of Congress Cataloging-in-Publication Data

Macht, Norman L. (Norman Lee), 1929–
Jim Abbott / Norman L. Macht.
p. cm.—(Great achievers)
Includes index.
ISBN 0-7910-2079-7
        0-7910-2092-4 (pbk)
1. Abbott, Jim, 1967– —Juvenile literature. 2. Baseball players—United States—
Biography—Juvenile literature. [1. Abbott, Jim, 1967– . 2. Baseball players.
3. Physically handicapped.] I. Title. II. Series: Great achievers (Chelsea House
Publishers)
GV865.A26M33 1994   93-31838
796.357'092—dc20   CIP
[B]   AC

CONTENTS

GREAT ACHIEVERS

LIVES OF THE PHYSICALLY CHALLENGED

A Message for Everyone

Jerry Lewis

Just 44 years ago—when I was the ripe old age of 23—an incredible stroke of fate rocketed me to overnight stardom as an entertainer. After the initial shock wore off, I began to have a very strong feeling that, in return for all life had given me, I must find a way of giving something back. At just that moment, a deeply moving experience in my personal life persuaded me to take up the leadership of a fledgling battle to defeat a then little-known group of diseases called muscular dystrophy, as well as other related neuromuscular diseases—all of which are disabling and, in the worst cases, cut life short.

In 1950, when the Muscular Dystrophy Association (MDA)—of which I am national chairman—was established, physical disability was looked on as a matter of shame. Franklin Roosevelt, who guided America through World War II from a wheelchair, and Harold Russell, the World War II hero who lost both hands in battle, then became an Academy Award–winning movie star and chairman of the President's Committee on Employment of the Handicapped, were the exceptions. One of the reasons that muscular dystrophy and related diseases were so little known was that people who had been disabled by them were hidden at home, away from the pity and discomfort with which they were generally regarded by society. As I got to know and began working with people who have disabilities, I quickly learned what a tragic mistake this perception was. And my determination to correct this terrible problem soon became as great as my commitment to see disabling neuromuscular diseases wiped from the face of the earth.

I have long wondered why it never occurs to us, as we experience the knee-jerk inclination to feel sorry for people who are physically disabled, that lives such as those led by President Roosevelt, Harold Russell, and all of the extraordinary people profiled in this Great Achievers series demonstrate unmistakably how wrong we are. Physical disability need not be something that blights life and destroys opportunity for personal fulfillment and accomplishment. On the contrary, as people such as Ray Charles, Stephen Hawking, and Ron Kovic prove, physical disability can be a spur to greatness rather than a condemnation of emptiness.

In fact, if my experience with physically disabled people can be taken as a guide, as far as accomplishment is concerned, they have a slight edge on the rest of us. The unusual challenges they face require finding greater-than-average sources of energy and determination to achieve much of what able-bodied people take for granted. Often, this ultimately translates into a lifetime of superior performance in whatever endeavor people with disabilities choose to pursue.

If you have watched my Labor Day Telethon over the years, you know exactly what I am talking about. Annually, we introduce to tens of millions of Americans people whose accomplishments would distinguish them regardless of their physical conditions—top-ranking executives, physicians, scientists, lawyers, musicians, and artists. The message I hope the audience receives is not that these extraordinary individuals have achieved what they have by overcoming a dreadful disadvantage that the rest of us are lucky not to have to endure. Rather, I hope our viewers reflect on the fact that these outstanding people have been ennobled and strengthened by the tremendous challenges they have faced.

In 1992, MDA, which has grown over the past four decades into one of the world's leading voluntary health agencies, established a personal achievement awards program to demonstrate to the nation that the distinctive qualities of people with disabilities are by no means confined to the famous. What could have been more appropriate or timely in that year of the implementation of the 1990 Americans with Disabilities Act than to take an action that could perhaps finally achieve the alteration of public perception of disability, which MDA had struggled over four decades to achieve?

On Labor Day, 1992, it was my privilege to introduce to America MDA's inaugural national personal achievement award winner, Steve Mikita, assistant attorney general of the state of Utah. Steve graduated magna cum laude from Duke University as its first wheelchair student in history and was subsequently named the outstanding young lawyer of the year by the Utah Bar Association. After he spoke on the Telethon with an eloquence that caused phones to light up from coast to coast, people asked me where he had been all this time and why they had not known of him before, so deeply impressed were they by him. I answered that he and thousands like him have been here all along. We just have not adequately *noticed* them.

It is my fervent hope that we can eliminate indifference once and for all and make it possible for all of our fellow citizens with disabilities to gain their rightfully high place in our society.

On Facing Challenges

John Callahan

I was paralyzed for life in 1972, at the age of 21. A friend and I were driving in a Volkswagen on a hot July night, when he smashed the car at full speed into a utility pole. He suffered only minor injuries. But my spinal cord was severed during the crash, leaving me without any feeling from my diaphragm downward. The only muscles I could move were some in my upper body and arms, and I could also extend my fingers. After spending a lot of time in physical therapy, it became possible for me to grasp a pen.

I've always loved to draw. When I was a kid, I made pictures of everything from Daffy Duck (one of my lifelong role models) to caricatures of my teachers and friends. I've always been a people watcher, it seems; and I've always looked at the world in a sort of skewed way. Everything I see just happens to translate immediately into humor. And so, humor has become my way of coping. As the years have gone by, I have developed a tremendous drive to express my humor by drawing cartoons.

The key to cartooning is to put a different spin on the expected, the normal. And that's one reason why many of my cartoons deal with the disabled: amputees, quadriplegics, paraplegics, the blind. The public is not used to seeing them in cartoons.

But there's another reason why my subjects are often disabled men and women. I'm sick and tired of people who presume to speak for the disabled. Call me a cripple, call me a gimp, call me paralyzed for life.

Just don't call me something I'm not. I'm not "differently abled," and my cartoons show that disabled people should not be treated any differently than anyone else.

All of the men, women, and children who are profiled in the Great Achievers series share this in common: their various handicaps have not prevented them from accomplishing great things. Their life stories are worth knowing about because they have found the strength and courage to develop their talents and to follow their dreams as fully as they can.

Whether able-bodied or disabled, a person must strive to overcome obstacles. There's nothing greater than to see a person who faces challenges and conquers them, regardless of his or her limitations.

Making his major league debut, 21-year-old Jim Abbott fires a pitch against the Seattle Mariners on April 8, 1989, in Anaheim. The left-hander threw 83 pitches, the fastest attaining 94 MPH, before he was taken out of the game.

1

"WELCOME TO THE BIG LEAGUES"

THE LONG SHADOWS AT Anaheim Stadium were fading in the California twilight as Jim Abbott strolled out to the bull pen to warm up at 6:30 on Saturday, April 8, 1989. Like any rookie pitcher making his first start in a major league game, the 21-year-old left-hander was a little nervous.

His parents, grandparents, and younger brother, Chad, had flown in from their home in Flint, Michigan, to cheer him on. But, to Abbott, that was a mixed blessing. Although he appreciated their support, he knew his mother was concerned that her presence when he pitched seemed to put a curse on him.

"I pitch well in front of my dad, but not my mom," he had told reporters a few days earlier. "I hate to say that, 'cause she'll freak out when she hears that. But it will be nice to have them here."

Anaheim Stadium, built in 1966 with a natural grass surface and a seating capacity of 64,593, is home to the California Angels of the American League.

Before heading for the bull pen, Abbott was surrounded by reporters asking the kinds of questions he was used to hearing. "Hopefully things will go well," he told them. "But if they don't, it won't be the end of the world."

He had no fear that he had to pitch well on this night or lose his place on the team. California Angels manager Doug Rader had assured him that he had won a place in the starting rotation, making the jump from college baseball to the majors.

The crowd that was rapidly filling Anaheim Stadium cheered as Abbott walked across the outfield grass toward the bull pen. For a young pitcher who had never pitched even a minor league game, this was unusual. What was more unusual, however, was that Jim Abbott did not take that long walk alone. This routine journey, taken by two starting pitchers before every game in every big league ballpark, is usually a solitary time for each pitcher to intensify his concentration for the challenge ahead of him. Jim Abbott was not allowed this quiet time. At least a dozen television cameramen, some from as far away as Japan, formed a jostling circle around him as he walked to the bull pen.

Abbott had been the center of this kind of attention all during spring training. He had won the Sullivan Award and other honors for amateur athletes while pitching at the University of Michigan in Ann Arbor, and he had pitched the gold-medal win for the U.S. team in the 1988 Olympics. Yet even these achievements did not warrant so much attention in the harsher, more demanding world of the major leagues. The reason this glaring spotlight shone on Jim Abbott had occurred 21 years and 7 months earlier, when the rookie pitcher was born without a right hand.

Many people are born with some physical shortcomings. But they do not grow up with the talent, heart, and courage to become big league ballplayers. More than 13,000 men had played major league baseball in the preceding 120 years. Only one—Hugh Daily—had been a one-handed pitcher, and he pitched in the 19th century. Jim Abbott's climb to this height made him—in other people's eyes—a freak, a novelty, or at least an oddity, like the bearded lady in a circus sideshow. But Abbott never thought of himself in the terms that others were quick to apply to him: disabled, handicapped, courageous, amazing.

"A handicap is a limitation," he said. "I haven't been limited in any way. I've been awfully fortunate in the things I've been given. I don't think there is anything special about me being in the major leagues. What I have done is not any more triumphant than anyone else's effort. I'm not special."

But no matter how much he tried to be just another pitcher, Abbott knew he could not escape the circus atmosphere that surrounded him. It had been that way ever since the day he pitched a no-hitter in a Little League game back in Flint and the newspapers began to write about the amazing one-handed pitcher.

So he was used to being seen as a novelty, and he did his best to put up with it. No word or gesture indicated that it upset or distracted him. He had seen so much of it that he could now retain his composure no matter how rudely it was tested. But nobody could be wholly un-affected by the persistent pressure of the endlessly re-peated questions. There had been so many requests for interviews during the week leading up to his debut that the Angels had been forced to hold a mammoth press confer-ence two days earlier.

By the time Abbott walked out to the mound to face the first batter of the Seattle Mariners, more than 46,000 people had filled the stadium. Everyone rooted for the quiet, fair-haired rookie to succeed. More than 150 report-ers—10 times the usual number of press corps—jammed into the press box.

The first batter, second baseman Harold Reynolds, re-membered the scene vividly. "When he was warming up, I marveled at what he was doing with his glove. 'Boy, that is something,' I said. 'How does he do that?' But when I stepped into the batters box, I was concentrating on the pitch, and all that other stuff left my mind. His first pitch was a strike and the big crowd let out a roar. It was like a play-off atmosphere. Then I grounded a single to right field. Did I feel like a villain for deflating his big moment? No. I stood on first base and thought, 'Okay. Welcome to the big leagues.'"

The next batter, Henry Cotto, lined a base hit, and Reynolds went to third. Abbott then bounced a pitch in the dirt that got by the catcher, and Cotto raced to second.

"There was definitely some nervousness there," Abbott later admitted. "Maybe I wasn't as clearly focused as I should have been. I wasn't rattled by the first two hits, but it made me realize I was in a battle."

There was also some nervousness in the private box of club owner Gene Autry, where Jim's family was sitting. His mother was chanting to herself, "If we can just get through three innings."

Abbott got the next three batters to ground out to second base, but his wild pitch had eliminated the chance for a double play, and two runs scored on the outs.

Although two balls were hit hard in the second inning, Abbott retired three in a row. In the third, some poor fielding behind him, a perfect bunt, and a walk loaded the bases, but a double play got him out of the inning. Now his nervous mother's mantra became, "Now if we can get through six more."

Meanwhile, the Mariners pitching ace, Mark Langston, was mowing down the Angels routinely. Abbott matched him in the fourth inning but ran into trouble in the fifth. With one out, Omar Vizquel singled. Reynolds hit a high bouncer that the second baseman booted. Abbott walked Cotto intentionally to load the bases.

Facing the left-hand batter Alvin Davis, Abbott fired a fastball right where he wanted it to go. Davis swung. His bat cracked in two. But the ball fluttered into right field just beyond everybody's reach, and two runs scored.

"Those kinds of plays are the most frustrating, the toughest to live with," Abbott said later.

An out and another hit scored two more runs, and the Mariners led, 6 to 0. Angels manager Doug Rader walked to the mound and waved in a relief pitcher. Abbott walked to the dugout amid a thunderous standing ovation. He had thrown 83 pitches, the fastest reaching 94 MPH.

Afterward, Rader was quick to bolster the young hurler's confidence. "We said beforehand that the number of pitches he threw and the number of innings he pitched would be determined by the amount of stress and duress that those pitches were thrown under. He'd been in a couple of jams. It was at the point where nothing more could be gained by him remaining in the game."

Rader also expressed the hope that the clamor around the one-handed rookie would subside. "I can't believe this poor guy's been going through all this. I'm sure he was churning inside, but he held it in."

The commotion continued after the game, and Abbott had to appear at a special press conference. With his parents present in the back of the room, he stood on a platform and patiently answered questions. "Over all, I'm a little disappointed," he said. "I wish I could do it over again. Maybe I was unnerved in my first start. I learned that, at this level, you can't just throw the ball over the plate. And you have to concentrate on every pitch. . . . In a few years, maybe I'll look back and say, 'It wasn't so bad.'. . . Maybe when I was warming up, I was caught up in the hoopla. The crowd support was a big deal for me. . . . I don't mind the extra attention, but I yearn for the day when I'm treated normally."

Jim Abbott was born without a right hand, but he had a fabulous left arm and a big heart. "I want to be known as a good baseball pitcher, not just as a good one-handed baseball pitcher," he said. "All I ever wanted was an opportunity."

Abbott transfers the ball from his glove to his left hand as he prepares to throw against a New York Yankees batter. In the more than 120 years of major league baseball, only two one-handed pitchers have made the grade for the majors—Hugh Daily, who pitched in the 19th century, and Jim Abbott, who began his major league career with the Angels in 1989.

In 1979, young Jim Abbott runs in from the mound during a Grant Hamady Midget League game in Flint, Michigan. By the time he was 11, Jim was averaging 12 strikeouts a game in Little League.

2

THE "HANDICAP"

JAMES ANTHONY ABBOTT was born on September 19, 1967, in South-field, Michigan. His parents, Mike and Kathy Abbott, were both 19, just out of high school. They had no warning that their baby would be anything but normal, so it came as a shock when they learned that Jim's right arm had not fully developed. It ended in a small, loose flap of skin about where his wrist should have been. One tiny nub of a finger dangled from the end of it.

When a baby is born with any kind of visible affliction, the parents are often concerned that there might be some unseen mental impairment as well. The Abbotts, however, were soon relieved to learn that Jim was healthy in all other respects.

The young couple rented an apartment in Flint. They had a plan for their future. Mike worked in a meat-packing plant and sold used cars; Kathy worked part-time and went to school at the University of

Michigan, Flint, where she earned a teaching degree. Then, while she taught adult education, Mike worked part-time and went to school to get his degree. Kathy went on to law school, and in 1990 became assistant city attorney in Flint. Mike became the sales manager for a beer distributor. Both parents knew the value of an education and passed that vision on to Jim and his brother, Chad, who was born when Jim was four.

Jim's parents faced an early decision, one they felt ill-equipped to make: should they raise Jim in a protective cocoon, warning him from the beginning that he was different, that he had a handicap that would limit the things he could do? This approach might spare him the pain and disappointment of trying to keep up with other kids on the playing fields and failing, or, even worse, being rejected and ridiculed by them. Or should they ignore his so-called disability as much as possible, encouraging Jim to do whatever he wanted to do and to find his own way to adapt to having only one hand?

They had no experience to guide them. But, like most young parents, they had no shortage of advice from family and friends. Still, the final decision was up to them. Relying more on instinct than experts' advice or how-to books, they chose to minimize the importance of Jim's physical defect and let him lead a normal life. If they did not make a big deal out of his not having a right hand, they hoped that he would not see it as a big deal either. It was an obstacle, a challenge to overcome, but no big deal.

Kids who are different from other children are often shy, probably because they do not wish to draw attention to their difference. But for as long as Jim could remember, his father urged him not to hesitate to meet people. "When you see someone new," Jim's father told him, "walk up to them shake their hand and say, 'Hi, my name is Jim Abbott.'"

Abbott credits this advice with shaping his outgoing nature. Growing up, he never felt self-conscious about his incomplete arm.

Jim showed an early interest in sports. He saw other children playing ball and decided that joining their games would help him be accepted by them. But he had to be able to perform on the field.

He learned to handle a ball and glove by playing catch with his father. Jim devised a way to catch the ball, remove his glove, and throw the ball, all with one hand. Before long he became adept at slipping the ball out of his glove as he dropped the glove or perched it on his right arm. Because he had never done it any other way, the maneuver came naturally to him. Once he had it down pat, he never had to change it.

"If there were times I got frustrated," he said, "it was because I wasn't doing something I knew I could do, not something I couldn't do."

When his dad was not there to play catch with him, Jim spent hours throwing a ball against a brick wall. As he practiced, he moved closer and closer to the wall, which forced him to slip his hand into the glove quicker to catch the ball bouncing back at him. He pitched imaginary games against the wall, pretending he was the great Nolan Ryan throwing smoke past helpless hitters.

The Abbotts moved to 923 Maxine Street, a pleasant residential street of two-storied houses. Their redbrick house with white trim and dark green shutters faced a street lined with huge maple trees that formed an umbrella of shade in the summer. A basketball hoop hung above the double garage doors. With his brother and Mark Conover, a pal who lived on the next street, Jim set up a batting cage in the backyard. Using a lawn chair for a backstop, a tennis ball, and a tiny bat, they took batting practice. A ball hit into the trees, scattering the squirrels, counted as a home run. Jim rested the end of the bat on his right arm and gripped it with his left hand.

By the time Jim was old enough to approach the kids playing ball, he felt confident that he could play almost any position and hold his own. Children can be cruel,

On June 1, 1975, Nolan Ryan smiles as he poses in the Angels dressing room at Anaheim Stadium after he pitched the fourth no-hitter of his career against the Baltimore Orioles. Jim admired Ryan, and whenever he pitched imaginary games against a brick wall, he pretended he was the "Ryan express" throwing fastballs.

however, and Jim took plenty of verbal shots. They teased him by saying his right "hand" looked like a foot. They called him Stub and Rag Arm and Crab. Sometimes the teasing sent him home crying. But his parents sent him right back out the next day with words of encouragement, and the tears soon stopped. In a home where there was never a negative word heard, Jim nurtured the positive attitude that he has carried with him toward every challenge he has faced.

Once he had demonstrated that he could play baseball as well as anybody else on the sandlots, the harassment stopped. The sideways looks and jeers and eyebrows raised in disbelief soon gave way to his being eagerly welcomed when it came time to choose up sides. Gradually the other children took no notice of Jim's "handicap."

No matter how much Jim wanted to act normal, there were still some things he could not do—cut paper with scissors, open a can, and cut a piece of meat—simple, everyday activities that most people do without any difficulty. When Jim was about four, a doctor persuaded the Abbotts to have him fitted with a prosthesis (an artificial device that replaces a missing part of the body), which was strapped to his right arm and ended in a metal hook. This artificial hand was supposed to enable Jim to do easy chores that required both hands. The metal hook, however, was heavy, ugly, and awkward, and it made Jim's difference more noticeable. His classmates called him Bionic Man and were afraid of the prosthesis. His teacher thought he might accidentally hurt someone with it. Jim hated it. It did not help him perform tasks better and certainly was no help on the ball field. In less than two years, he took the prosthesis off and announced that he wanted no part of it, ever again.

Despite their encouraging words, the Abbotts believed that Jim's baseball activity would be limited to playing catch and sandlot games. They tried to interest him in soccer, where only the goalie is allowed to use his hands. But Jim loved baseball more than any other sport, and there was nothing to do but continue to support him as far as his ability and courage would take him. In any case, they did not believe that would be very far.

Flint is a blue-collar, industrial city located about 70 miles northwest of Detroit. Although some factories have recently been closed, it is quite evident that Flint remains a General Motors town. The north-south I-475 highway is called UAW (United Auto Workers) Freeway; the east-west I-69 is named Chevrolet Buick Freeway. The residents of Flint are very sports-minded: anyone who roots for professional teams other than the Detroit Tigers, Lions,

A vintage photograph refers to Flint, Michigan, as Vehicle City. Flint, Abbott's hometown, is situated about 70 miles northwest of Detroit and is primarily known for its General Motors factories.

Jim and his father were ardent Detroit Tigers fans and Mike Abbott frequently drove his son to Tiger Stadium (shown here in 1968) to watch the team. After games, Jim liked to wait outside the players' gate to get autographs from his favorite ballplayers.

and Pistons is asking for trouble. The University of Michigan's Wolverine teams are also closely followed by residents.

Mike Abbott frequently took his son to baseball games at Tiger Stadium. Most games were played at night—it was usually well past 10:00 P.M. when the games ended—and Mike and Jim had a 90-minute drive home. Jim's father had to get up early the next morning to go to work, but Jim was an avid card and autograph collector, and he insisted on waiting outside the players' gate to get autographs. One night after the Detroit Tigers played the Boston Red Sox, Mike had urged Jim to start for home, but his son wanted especially to get Boston outfielder Jim Rice to sign a ball. It was late, almost midnight, and Mike Abbott was tired. The Red Sox's bus filled with players and Jim waited patiently. Finally, Rice came out of the stadium, and Jim held out the ball to him and asked, "Please, sir, would you sign this for me?" Without uttering a word, Rice pushed Jim out of the way and climbed into the bus.

Years later, Abbott would often remember this incident whenever he was asked to sign autographs for kids. He came to understand Rice's attitude better, however, when he felt the brunt of the pressure and the hounding that would try the patience of a saint or when meals could not be enjoyed without people shoving a dozen pictures or cards at him to sign.

In addition to their interest in college and professional sports, the people of Flint actively support sports programs for their own youth. Jim began with T-ball when he was six and progressed to the Midget League in the Greater Flint Youth Baseball Program. When he first signed up, he drew plenty of stares from other children, and coaches, too. But the program's motto was Every Kid Can Play. Whatever they thought of him, the coaches gave Jim the same chance as everybody else. That was all Jim ever asked for, a fair chance.

"Nobody ever suggested I should sit and keep score," he said. "If they had told me I couldn't play, anywhere along the line, I probably would have stopped. But nobody ever discouraged me. That was the key."

Jim enjoyed hitting, but he got bored with the lack of action when coaches stuck him in the outfield. So he became a pitcher and played first base whenever he was not pitching.

His strong left arm soon made everyone forget that he was lacking a right hand. In his first start, he pitched a no-hitter. By the age of 11, Jim was averaging 12 strikeouts in the five-inning games. But pitching demanded more fielding dexterity than did the outfield. Jim rested the glove on his right arm as he threw the pitch, then quickly slipped his left hand into it to be ready for a fielding play. When he caught a ball hit back to him, he dropped the glove, plucked the ball out of it, and threw to the base.

City park supervisor Dave Blight said, "He does it all so quickly, he is amazing. You really don't realize that he has only one hand."

Occasionally the maneuver failed. When that happened, Jim practiced extra hours. "He worked harder than

Jim Abbott signs autographs at R.F.K. Memorial Stadium in Washington, D.C., before a preseason game in April 1993. Because he remembers what it was like as a child to seek autographs from players only to be pushed aside, Abbott tries to oblige as many children as possible whenever he is asked for his autograph.

anyone I've ever seen," said his Little League coach, Jeff Blanchard.

"Jim never displayed any anger or frustration with his condition," Mike Abbott recalled, "although it certainly must have bothered him."

Coach Blanchard confirmed that Jim did not show any inhibition about his situation while on the field. "He'll even joke about it once in a while. And every guy on the team knows that he's the best player."

Kathy Abbott, on the other hand, sensed her son's impatience. "He never verbalized it, but you could see that sometimes it got to him. He doesn't have to say anything."

To his parents, Jim was just one of the kids playing ball and having a good time. They gave it no further thought, and they had no notion that it might amount to anything more than that. Then, on Sunday, July 15, 1979, they read a long story about their son in the *Flint Journal*. The star pitcher for the Grant Hamady Midget League team, Jim had won six games without allowing a single earned run. He had struck out 74 batters in 32 innings and given up only 5 hits. He was also hitting .562. Jim, who was now a student at Whittier Junior High, played it all down. "[My parents] don't want me to get bigheaded," he told the reporter. "Whenever I get too impressed with myself, I try to remember that I didn't get here single-handedly."

While no one else saw any future for the 11-year-old beyond Flint, Jim himself had aspirations. Asked about major leaguers who had been an inspiration to him, he said, "I look at them and wish it was me."

His parents were surprised to learn how good a player Jim was. After reading the newspaper, Mike Abbott turned to his wife and said, "Well, we better get down there and see him pitch."

As Jim worked his way up through higher levels of competition, coaches told the Abbotts that each level would be as far as their son could go. "With every step we thought about whether it would catch up to him,"

Mike Abbott said. "At what level would his peers take over?"

There was no doubt that Jim could throw hard, but there were always questions about his fielding ability. When he was in the ninth grade, he pitched a game in which a leadoff batter bunted on him and reached first base safely. The next five or six batters bunted, too, but Jim threw each of the hitters out. Jim did not mind being tested this way; if batters were foolish enough to turn themselves into easy outs, that was okay with him. Still, no matter how often he passed such tests, doubts about his fielding ability persisted each time he pitched.

One of the doubters was Bob Holec, the baseball coach at Flint's Central High School, who wondered if Jim could handle a ball hit sharply back at him by bigger, stronger batters in varsity competition.

One day he sat with Mike Abbott watching Jim pitch the junior varsity city championship game. As they discussed Jim's fielding, a batter hit a high hopper sharply back to the mound. Jim slipped his hand into the glove in time to snare the ball and throw the batter out at first. The two men looked at each other. The discussion—and misgivings—ended.

Repeatedly, Jim, seen here in a game for the Indians of Flint Central High School, had to prove to batters and to coaches that he could field balls as well as anyone.

Jim was aware of the questions and the doubts. Later, when reporters asked him how he would cope with a hard line drive aimed at his head, Jim would say, "Just like any other pitcher; I'd duck."

He did not resent the experts' skepticism as long as they gave him a chance to prove himself. He did, however, resent being blamed when a batter beat out a perfect bunt that nobody could have fielded in time or when he made an error that was attributed to his one-handedness. The few times that he dropped his glove in making the switch from hand to right arm, people shook their heads and wrote off any chances of his going further. Nevertheless, the cynicism did not discourage Jim Abbott.

On November 10, 1984, quarterback Jim Abbott leads Flint Central to a 26–20 victory over Midland High in Michigan's Class A football play-offs. In the first half of the game, Abbott hurled four touchdown passes and completed passes for a total of 199 yards. It was a sportswriter's report of Abbott's quarterbacking in this game that brought Abbott national attention.

3

NATIONAL FAME— FROM FOOTBALL

AFTER JIM ABBOTT established himself as Central High's varsity pitching ace in his sophomore year, most people in Flint accepted him as he was and gave no more thought to his not having a right hand. But there were still some strangers who came out to see the one-handed pitcher whom they had heard so much about. Coach Holec recalled one man who came to a game out of curiosity. "It took him three innings to figure out which player he had come to see, because Jim made the switch with his glove so smoothly."

When he was not pitching, Abbott played the outfield or first base—and once took the field at shortstop. He made every play that each position demanded; one day he even threw out a baserunner at home plate after chasing down a long fly ball in left center. Abbott made the all-city team in 1983.

Abbott attended Flint Central High School and established himself as the varsity pitching ace in his sophomore year.

Mark Conover, Abbott's friend from their grammar school days, was Central's shortstop. Both boys had ambitions of playing professional ball. One's successes spurred the other to do better in a friendly competition. One day they made a bet and solemnly drew up a contract between them. Conover recalled the terms: "If he turned pro he was to buy me a car, and if I turned pro, I would buy him one." Later, Conover, an outstanding hockey player, had four knee operations as a result of injuries he received on the ice, putting an end to his baseball hopes. "I don't let Jim forget about that bet," he said, "but I'm still waiting."

Baseball was always Abbott's first love, so it is ironic that his earliest national notoriety came from football. In August 1983, Central High's football coach, Joe Eufinger, had a dilemma. He had a good quarterback, Randy Levels, for his team, but he had no backup in case Levels was injured. Eufinger talked over his problem with Bob Holec, who doubled as the offensive coach. They agreed that Abbott was the best all-around athlete at Central High. His father had been a high school football star. Jim Abbott certainly had the arm to throw a pass, so they decided to ask him to come out for the team. Abbott had never given any thought to playing football. He played in touch football games just for pleasure and even played some basketball, but playing baseball was his foremost interest. Football looked like a fun sport, and as a lark Abbott joined the late August workouts.

The most difficult move he had to learn was handing off to a running back. "A quarterback handing off to his left will normally use his right hand to slap the ball into the runner's midsection," Eufinger explained. "Jim couldn't do that. He had to put the ball into the runner with his left hand and get the hand out of the way in time to avoid a fumble. I figured if a kid can throw a baseball, put a glove on, catch the ball, get the glove off, get the ball in his hand, and throw a guy out, he could figure out how to twist his hand in handing off a football. And he did."

Abbott practiced taking the snap from center and handling the ball. The center placed the ball into Abbott's hand, then Abbott would steady it with his right arm as he brought it up to his chest and gripped it by the laces.

Abbott hands off the ball to a teammate during the Flint Central–Midland play-off game. One of the most difficult moves he had to learn in playing football was handing off to a running back.

Abbott saw a few minutes of playing time that fall, completing two of nine passes for 30 yards.

In the spring of 1984, Abbott continued to fan the hitters with his pitches, striking out 14 in 59 innings. His fastball was clocked at 80 MPH. Abbott, however, struggled with his control and with himself. He had become a perfection-ist and felt he had failed every time he walked a batter or gave up a hit. After a game in which Central was beaten by Bay City Western, 3 to 1, Abbott berated himself, "I just shouldn't have hung that curve ball."

When school was out, he pitched for Flint Grossi in the Connie Mack League. Wherever he played, he attracted more attention than any other player, but he was so well liked by everyone that there was no jealousy. Grossi coach Ted Mahan recalled, "When Jim pitched the team got a little more excited because they wanted to do a little better for him. The three years I had him he lost so many tight games, 1 to 0 and 2 to 1, because I think our guys got too hyped up."

In Abbott's final year in the Connie Mack League, the team came within one out of going to the Connie Mack World Series. "That was one of the bitterest memories I

Abbott's fastball was clocked at 80 MPH in 1984. Although he struggled with his control, he became a perfectionist and felt that he had failed every time he walked a batter or gave up a hit.

Abbott cheers on a teammate during a baseball game in 1984. Although he attracted more attention at games than the other players, Abbott was admired by his fellow teammates and they did not seem to harbor any resentment toward him.

could ever have," Abbott said. "I wanted to go so bad and I was on the mound and we lost."

Abbott lifted weights during the off-season. He grew taller and stronger and more confident that he could succeed at every level of the game. At 16, he was now 6 feet 4 inches tall and weighed 175 pounds.

Abbott went out for football again in August 1984. During one of the plays in a practice game, quarterback Randy Levels was injured. Playing at half speed, he and Abbott alternated plays for the first two games of the season. When Levels returned to full-time action, Abbott sat on the bench.

Abbott's baseball dreams—and more—almost came to a screeching halt one Saturday when he and a bunch of his buddies drove to nearby Ann Arbor to see the Michigan Wolverines football team play a Big Ten game. After the game, the six friends climbed into their car and set off to visit a friend's sister who lived in the area.

"We were not speeding," Central High offensive lineman Mike Staisil recalled, "but rounding a curve on I-96, the tire hit a rut on the side of the road and our weight tipped the small car and we rolled over four or five times onto the median and landed upside down on the other edge. One more roll would have taken us into the other traffic lane. Jim was in the front seat. The driver was thrown from the car and broke a leg. Mark Conover broke his collarbone. The car was totaled, but Jim and I escaped unharmed. There were ambulances all over the place. A state policeman said there was no way any of us should have survived."

The accident occurred a few weeks before the game against Central's biggest rivals, Northern High, for the city championship and a berth in the state play-offs. A few days before the big game with Northern, the team was stunned by the news that Randy Levels had barely missed the minimum grade level needed to play, and he was declared ineligible. It was up to Abbott to quarterback. Staisil and Abbott had been taking some honor courses at Northern, so they knew the football players there. "When we got there on the Friday morning before our big game with them," Staisil recalled, "they were waiting for us. Some of the players had pulled socks over their right hands, to make it look like they didn't have a right hand. It was their way of trying to ride us."

The ruse did not work; Central easily beat Northern, 43 to 14. "I have a lot of friends in Northern," Abbott said after the game. "Beating them really felt good."

The quarterback also did the punting for the team, and Abbott was their best punter, averaging 37 yards a kick. (Abbott punted with his right foot, which might indicate that he was a natural-born right-hander.) Once a bad snap went over his head. He jumped up and caught it and got a booming kick away that brought a roar from the crowd.

The Central Indians' first challenge in the play-offs was undefeated Midland, which had beaten them 16 to 13 during the season. During the first quarter of the game, it did not take long for the white number 21 on the back of Abbott's red jersey to become green from grass stains. The Central Indians had no running attack, and consequently Abbott was always under pressure from two or three pass rushers. He was flat on his back when many of his passes were caught. In the second quarter, with the score 7 to 7, Central had the ball, third and 11 on their own 19-yard line. As Abbott faded back to pass, an onrushing lineman cracked into him just as he got the ball away. Down they went; Abbott, still on the ground, grabbed his right arm in pain. He did not see David Burks catch the pass for a 34-yard gain. Abbott went to the sidelines, but after just one play, he ran back onto the field to the lusty applause of the home crowd.

"It took some guts to come into that football situation and take over," coach Eufinger said. "He never thought about getting hurt; it never occurred to him that anything could happen to threaten his pitching hopes. He never hesitated to run with the ball or scramble to get away from the pass rush. In one game he made the tackle on a guy who had intercepted a pass."

Abbott led the Central Indians down the field and threw his second touchdown pass. He threw for two more touchdowns in the second quarter as Central built up a 26–7 lead at halftime. It rained during the second half, but Abbott never fumbled. Midland came back strong, but Central held on to win, 26 to 20. Abbott threw 4 touchdown passes and completed 15 of 23 for 239 yards. He gave credit to his receivers and blockers but quipped, "I guess we beat them single-handedly. It was one of the best experiences I've ever had as an athlete. . . . A lot of my family and friends came to see me play. It was really great to share it with them."

After the Midland game, a Detroit sportswriter penned a story about the amazing one-handed quarterback at Flint Central. Newspapers all over the country picked up the report. As a result, a CBS television crew showed up, and sportscaster Irv Cross interviewed Abbott, David Burks, and Mike Staisil. The feature was shown at halftime during the annual Thanksgiving Day game of the Detroit Lions; millions of turkey-stuffed families watched the interview on their television sets.

"We always looked at Jim as a normal guy," Staisil said. "Never thought of him as being special or having a handi-cap. His gift was motivation and wanting to excel."

The quest for a state championship ended the following Saturday when Ann Arbor Pioneer beat Central, 14 to 7. Jim threw one touchdown pass, but Pioneer intercepted him six times.

"Jim was all the offense we had," coach Eufinger said, "and they knew it. They set up a lot of different defenses against him, and Jim's inexperience cost him. But he enjoyed every minute of his football experience." For the year, Abbott completed 45 of 92 passes for 604 yards.

On January 11, 1985, Abbott was honored as the March of Dimes amateur athlete of the year at a dinner in the Pontiac Silverdome. He sat beside another award winner, Detroit Tigers pitcher Milt Wilcox, who had won 18 games in 1984. At the time, Wilcox represented all of Abbott's ambitions.

In high school, the social life of Abbott and his friends was almost as regimented as football practice. On Friday and Saturday nights, five or six of them would meet for debating and cruising. The script never varied. The first big debate was over who would drive. Nobody wanted the job because the driver got stuck with buying the gas, and he was the only one who could not relax and cut up and laugh; he had to keep his eyes on the road. They settled that issue by playing rock, paper, and scissors; the loser drove.

The next argument dealt with who would get to ride in the front seat. Once they got under way, the endless dis-cussion began over where to go. For hours they badgered the poor driver: "Turn here . . . no, go that way . . . let's go

Angelo's, known for its Coney Island, is a popular restaurant in Flint. Abbott and his high school buddies were regular customers at Angelo's, where they ordered Coneys, cheese-burgers, and shakes.

there . . . Naah, let's not go there. . . let's go there instead." It was a ceremony played out as predictably as a religious rite, usually to the music of Bruce Springsteen. In the end, they never went anywhere but always wound up at Angelo's, where they would meet the same group of five or six girls every time.

Flint is known for the Coney Island, a hot dog (made with sheep casing for crunchiness) with chili and onions, and Angelo's is its shrine. Open almost around the clock, Angelo's is jammed with business suits and blue jeans alike at midday, but it belongs to the students in the evening. "All the kids went there," Joe Eufinger said. "It was the serious grease intake place on the east side of town."

But Abbott and Staisil did not go for the Coneys. "We always ordered cheeseburgers and chocolate shakes," Staisil said, "and split an order of fries with brown gravy. The gravy made the fries sort of soggy, and of course we always had to add ketchup to them, too. Our parents always knew where we'd been; they could smell the grease on us when we got home."

As is true for many teenagers, their social life revolved around food, with rules as fixed as the course of the planets around the sun. They went to the Halo Burger downtown, a daytime stop only, for QPs—quarter pounders. The deluxe Halo Burger had green olives and mayonnaise on it.

The gang also went to Rizzo's, across from Central High, for pizza by the slice, but that was strictly after school. School was out at 1:30 P.M., and football practice did not begin until 3:00 P.M., so they went to Rizzo's whenever they did not raid the fridge at Jim Abbott's house, a few blocks away.

The PX Barbeque for ribs was reserved for family dining. It was the only place where Abbott needed help, to separate the racks of bones. (The PX eventually went out of business, the only regular hangout of the group's that no longer exists.)

In high school, Jim's favorite subjects were history and English. He was an avid reader and still is. Abbott did not care for math. In his senior year, he made the National Honor Society and won the Red & Black Award, the school's highest honor, for scholastic and athletic excellence. The five-foot trophy he was given bears his name along with the names of the previous winners of the award.

Jim was an overpowering pitcher as a senior. With his fastball reaching 90 MPH, he pitched the first of four no-hitters on opening day, striking out 16 in the seven-inning game. On May 3, he fanned 9 of the first 10 he faced in the opener of the Greater Flint Tournament. Three days later, after he struck out 13 of the 15 batters he faced in a five-inning no-hitter, the coach of the other team said, "This isn't fair."

By now, major league scouts were in the stands at every game and the publicity blitz began in earnest. An NBC television crew showed up for a Connie Mack League game. Then a Toronto TV station did a feature on Abbott at the Greater Flint All-Star Game. When he pitched the Indians into the finals, 2 to 0, and hit a double and triple, there were 50 media people in the crowd, and scouts from the major league teams of the Phillies, Blue Jays, Mets, Cubs, Tigers, and Royals.

A 3–2 loss, in which Abbott relieved and hit a home run, ended hopes of a state title. Four days later, Central played

Flushing for the Greater Flint championship. A record crowd of 1,500 jammed into Flint's 500-seat Whaley Park. Abbott started and was in trouble throughout the game. His control was rocky. Six times he walked the leadoff man, but each time he reached back and showed the heart of a gamer, one who is plucky and unyielding. Nonetheless, Flushing managed to score, and that was enough for a 1–0 win. Once again, the big win had eluded Abbott.

Scouts admired Abbott's fastball and his toughness, but most of them still raised the same old questions: could he field well enough, and could a one-handed pitcher make it in the big leagues? Many high school whizzes with two hands never made it.

Toronto scout Don Welke was one of the few who had no doubts. He saw a popping fastball and a big league heart. He also saw beyond the strikeouts to the tenacity and the fierce desire to be perfect on every pitch. A thrown glove once impressed him more than a thrown pitch, when he saw Abbott fling his glove to the ground in disgust with himself for having given up a base hit. Doubts about Abbott's fielding ability did not matter to Welke.

Coach Holec agreed. "Everybody looks at his bad arm and forgets he has a good arm. He has tremendous upper body strength. . . . He's just a tremendous athlete. He's been handed so much pressure in the last year. He's been on national television with Phil Donahue, 'Good Afternoon, Detroit.' . . . He thrives on this pressure. This has separated him from good to great. But there is no jealousy on the team because of his success. Except the coach is jealous."

Abbott averaged more than two strikeouts per inning and batted cleanup (that is, fourth), hitting .427 with 10 stolen bases and 7 home runs, many of them banging off the field house wall, 400 feet from home plate.

Named to the all-state team, Abbott traveled to Chicago to play a similar team from Illinois. The players all went to Wrigley Field to watch the Chicago Cubs play the New

In a pivotal game in 1985, Abbott hit a double and a triple and pitched the Central Indians into the finals, 2 to 0.

York Mets. Abbott was awed by the pitching of New York's Dwight "Doc" Gooden that day.

But the Detroit Tigers were Abbott's team, and veteran shortstop Alan Trammell was the player he most admired. Trammell represented the type of player Abbott wanted to be: one who is quiet, avoids publicity and the celebrity limelight, and just does his job consistently everyday all season, then disappears from view until the next spring. But Abbott knew that anonymity would be impossible for him. He also admired Detroit pitcher Dan Petry and was fascinated by Lance Parrish's catcher's mitt with the big orange circle around its perimeter. He focused on that glove for years, watching Parrish warm up Detroit pitchers.

Abbott began helping children who had similar physical problems during his high school days. One day he met 10-year-old Greg Norneber in Bay City when Central traveled there for a game. Greg had been born without a left hand. Using a prosthesis, Greg played center field for a Little League minor team. Abbott played catch with him and told him, "You can do whatever you want to do. There is no limit." Abbott said afterward, "Any time I can help another youngster like me, that makes playing ball worthwhile." No matter how many children were brought before him, Abbott never shunned talking to them.

With all its troubles following the closing of a large General Motors factory and the reputation of being the worst city in the country because of its high crime rate, Flint needed someone of whom it could feel proud. Jim Abbott became that person. *Flint Journal* columnist John Gooch wrote that Abbott was the best pitcher the Flint area had seen in many years.

When Abbott graduated from high school in June 1985, he became eligible to be drafted by a major league team. Round after round, he was passed by. Finally, in the 36th round, the Toronto Blue Jays picked Abbott.

The Blue Jays invited Abbott to Toronto in August to pitch batting practice and offered him a $50,000 bonus and guarantees of a college education. During his weekend in Toronto, Abbott began to believe that he could, in fact, pitch professionally. His initial reaction to the offer was, "This is what I want; I'm going to take it."

During a Toronto press conference with Abbott, Blue Jays broadcaster Tony Kubek (who later became the New York Yankees sportscaster) recalled:

> Some people were amazed that he had the audacity to think he could pitch in the big leagues. There were some awkward moments at the press conference. Somebody stood up and said, "But, Jim, uh . . . you have a . . . a handicap . . . you, uh, umm, don't have a . . . hand. . . . What if they bunt on you?" It was a logical question but a tough one to ask. Jim looked the guy in the eye and said simply, "I'll throw him out."

Jim Abbott had two ambitions, however. One was to be a big league pitcher and the other was to pitch for his favorite college team, the Michigan Wolverines. His parents had always stressed the importance of education. They knew that, no matter how much ability their son had, baseball could not be counted on to guarantee long-term success or employment. Injuries and bad luck could hurt anyone's chances, and if he could not be a pitcher he wanted to be a teacher.

Abbott turned down the Toronto offer and enrolled at the University of Michigan in Ann Arbor. He was merely postponing one ambition so he could achieve both.

There remained many people who believed Abbott had gone as far as he could go in baseball, considering his "difference." Still, Abbott had his own definition of being different; he would be different by becoming a great pitcher.

Starting pitcher Jim Abbott jumps for joy after the U.S. team wins the gold medal in baseball at the Summer Olympic Games in Seoul, South Korea, on September 28, 1988.

4

WINNING THE GOLD

WHEN JIM ABBOTT arrived at the University of Michigan campus in Ann Arbor in the fall of 1985, he had all the normal fears of any college freshman. College presented a higher level of academic challenge and athletic competition than he had ever faced. Abbott believed that he belonged where he was, and he had the determination to succeed.

As soon as he arrived in Ann Arbor, the media bombardment intensified. The networks ABC, CNN, and ESPN televised features on him, and the "Phil Donahue Show" invited him to appear as a guest. Newspaper stories called Abbott an example to other youngsters with one hand or arm, but he did not feel inspirational. He was just himself, doing what he could with what he had. He certainly did not feel very special when he tried to button the buttons on his left sleeve, for example, and had to ask his mother or roommate to do it for him.

In the spring of 1986, the Wolverines traveled to Florida in search of warm weather to get ready for the Big Ten season. Abbott quickly learned that playing college ball was a big step up from high school. On March 7, he started against Villanova University. After striking out the first batter, he was rocked for three runs before being taken out. But he gained his first win without retiring a batter on March 18. North Carolina led, 3 to 2, in the eighth, and had a man on third with two outs when Abbott came on in relief. He threw two quick strikes, and then the Tarheels flashed the sign for the runner to steal home as the catcher threw the ball back to Abbott on the mound. Abbott took the throw, deftly perched the glove on his right arm as he slipped the ball out of it, and threw home in time to get the runner. Michigan rallied in the ninth to win it. "I can see why they try things like that," Abbott said. "But, to me, it's an easy out."

In his first appearance at Fisher Stadium on the U. of M. campus, Abbott worked the last four innings of a combined no-hitter started by Scott Kamieniecki, his road roommate. In that game he made a putout at first base, nabbed a bunt pop fly in foul ground, and speared a high chopper over the mound. When he shut out Western Michigan, 1 to 0, in the last preseason game, ESPN named Abbott amateur athlete of the week. The constant demands for interviews and appearances had begun and would never let up during Abbott's three years at Michigan.

The Big Ten is a tough athletic arena; many of its players go on to star in the big leagues. In the spotlight of national TV, Abbott relieved against Minnesota on April 7, and took the 7–2 loss. Five days later he lost a gain, 9 to 7, to Purdue. After that he won six in a row, but he sometimes struggled with his control. Questions about his fielding subsided; Abbott fielded everything hit back to him and made only one error, on a wild pickoff throw.

In the Big Ten championship game, Minnesota took a
4–3 lead in the third. Abbott came in, plunked the first
batter he faced with a pitch, then set down 15 in a row,
fanning 10, and won, 9 to 5. The Wolverines, however, did
not make it to the College World Series, having lost early
on to Oral Roberts University in the Mideast Regional
play-offs.

In the summer of 1986, Abbott pitched in a city amateur
league. His team lost the state tournament, but Abbott was
asked by a Detroit team to pitch for them in a national
tourney in Johnstown, Pennsylvania. Before a crowd of
10,000 he struck out 15 and won, 2 to 1.

Abbott's success as a freshman brought increased
attention from scouts in his second year and still more
demands for interviews. He received letters calling him
"inspirational," a "hero," and "courageous," but he did
not feel he was any of these things. All he did was pitch.
Although it took time to respond to the letters and to
visit and talk to kids, he did not mind doing these
activities if he was truly helping someone overcome a
problem.

The list of awards for amateur athletes that he would
eventually win over the years began in January 1987, when
Abbott was named Most Courageous Athlete for 1986 by
the Philadelphia Sports Writers Association. Although he
graciously accepted this and all the honors that followed,
Abbott was uncomfortable with being singled out for
doing what had come naturally to him all his life. "I pitch
to win," he said, "not to be courageous."

Abbott was not sharp in his first start as a sophomore,
losing 8 to 0 to Oklahoma. But after he had his 90-plus
MPH fastball humming and he honed his control, he reeled
off nine straight wins, including a one-hitter against Illinois. During one stretch, he pitched 31 straight shutout
innings. In the Big Ten tournament, he lost the opener, 9
to 4, to Iowa but came back two days later to defeat Purdue,
as the Wolverines won their second straight conference

title. Abbott finished with an 11-3 record and 2.03 ERA. He made only two errors.

Abbott's success and the flood of national publicity earned him an invitation to try out for the U.S. team in the Pan-American Games of 1987. (Held every four years, one year before the Olympics, the Pan-American Games are open to amateur athletes of both sexes from the nations of North America, Central America, South America, and the Caribbean.) But the skepticism over how far a one-handed pitcher could go as the competition got tougher was still hounding Abbott.

Ron Fraser, the University of Miami coach who invited Abbott to the Pan-American Games, admitted that he did it more out of curiosity than anything else. "I didn't take it serious," Fraser said. "I knew the competition would be the best in the world, better than college teams."

Fraser had the same doubts about Abbott's fielding ability. In practice, Fraser ordered hitters to bunt on Abbott, who fielded all of the bunts cleanly. "He proved me wrong," Fraser conceded.

The other players at the Pan-American tryouts were also curious, but after the first few days together, they no longer noticed that there was anything different about Abbott. "He treated it all so lightly," recalled pitcher Jim Poole, "we forgot about it, except when he fooled around boxing with some guys. Then he taped up the stump and jabbed with it, and it made a hard weapon."

Abbott benefited from the coaching staff; he learned to throw a slider from Georgia Tech coach Jim Morris, a pitch he later relied on at the 1988 Olympics.

Among the national baseball teams that participated in the Pan-American Games, Cuba was the perennial favorite to win. At Cuba's invitation, Fraser took Team USA to Havana for a seven-game practice series.

Inquisitive Cuban fans flocked around Abbott at the hotel and at the beach where the team stopped one day.

Youngsters followed him wherever he went but Abbott took his popularity in stride.

Cuban baseball fans are as fanatic as any in the world, and they take great pride in their national team. No American team had beaten a Cuban team in 25 years.

The 55,000-seat Havana Stadium was filled to overflowing on the night Abbott pitched. President Fidel Castro, who was considered a good pitcher during his youth, attended the game. The Cubans had already beaten Team USA's top pitchers and they looked forward to an easy victory over the one-handed pitcher. The crowd's good-natured tolerance turned to admiration and then to a standing ovation as Abbott set down the Cuban hitters before leaving with an 8–3 lead in the seventh inning.

After the game, Castro came down to meet Abbott and patted him on the head. Abbott compared the Cuban leader to Michigan football coach Bo Schembechler. "They both have that presence, that dictator kind of air about them. I had the same feeling the first time I met both of them. They kind of intimidate you just by being in the room."

But the Cuban experience was not all fun. One player got sick from the food or water and spent the entire time recuperating in the hospital. That cast a warning to the others; they were very careful about what they ate and drank. "The only liquids available were orange soda and carbonated waters," remarked Gregg Olson, who was Abbott's roommate on the trip and who later became a pitcher for the Baltimore Orioles. "We got tired of the soda, and we'd shake the water bottles to get the fizz out before we could drink it." Olson said he lived on bread and rice for a week.

At the end of their stay, the U.S. players flew back to Miami. Landing at 2:00 A.M., the players headed for the nearest place open—Denny's—where they gulped down pitchers of water and devoured hamburgers. "It was strange being so eager for a good drink of water," teammate Jim Poole explained.

"I was sick as a dog for two days after," Olson declared.

The 1987 Pan-American Games took place in Indianapolis, Indiana, and were televised around the world. On August 7, the night before the opening ceremonies, an official stopped Abbott and informed him that the captains of all the U.S. teams had chosen him to carry their flag in the procession.

"Certainly this is a big thrill," Abbott told reporters, "probably the biggest of all. You get a chance to represent

Abbott carries the U.S. flag during the opening ceremony of the Pan-American Games on August 8, 1987. Abbott was overjoyed about being selected to lead the U.S. athletes in the parade and said, "You get a chance to represent your country and be the one person out of 700 to carry the flag. It's something I'll always remember."

your country and be the one person out of 700 to carry the flag. It's something I'll always remember."

With his family in the stands, Abbott led the U.S. contingent, the last of the 38 nations represented, as the U.S. athletes marched onto the Indianapolis Speedway.

In the Pan-American Games, Abbott's pitching enabled Team USA to beat Nicaragua, 18 to 0. Abbott came out of the bull pen to pitch four innings in a 7–6 win over Canada to put the United States into the finals against Cuba. But he could not pitch again with so little rest, and the favored Cuban team won the game for the gold medal. Team USA's silver medal finish clinched a place in the 1988 Olympics, and Abbott's 8 and 1 record assured him consideration for the U.S. Olympic team.

Abbott's studies at Michigan that fall and winter were frequently interrupted. On October 8, 1987, he went to New York with his father and U. of M. coach Bud Middaugh to accept the Golden Spikes Award, the equivalent of college football's Heisman Trophy, as the top amateur baseball player in the country. There he met Will Clark, the San Francisco Giants first baseman, who had previously won the award. Abbott asked Clark how much tougher it was in the major leagues than in college baseball. Clark told him, "There isn't that much difference. The arms are a little better, the speed and the pitching, and they don't make as many mistakes." Just work at it, he told Abbott, who went off later in the month to St. Louis, Missouri, to watch the World Series, thinking the big leagues were not that far away.

In March 1988, Abbott and his parents returned to Indianapolis when he was nominated for the Amateur Athletic Union's prestigious Sullivan Award, given each year to the top amateur athlete in all sports. They went to the dinner expecting one of the world-record holders, such as track-and-field athlete Jackie Joyner-Kersee or diver Greg Louganis, to win. Besides, no baseball player had ever been presented with the Sullivan Award. Conse-

In New York, Abbott poses with the 10th Golden Spikes Award at a ceremony in which he was honored as the nation's outstanding amateur player on October 8, 1987.

Abbott holds the Sullivan Award after it was presented to him on March 7, 1988, by the Amateur Athletic Union (AAU). The award is given annually to the nation's outstanding amateur athlete.

quently, they were all stunned when they heard that Jim had been announced as the winner.

As he accepted the trophy, Abbott said, "I think they picked the worst athlete up here." Then he added, "My mom kept me from turning pro, and it is nights like tonight that make me glad I made that decision."

Later Kathy Abbott told reporters, "We always like to say we never held him back from anything, but there were times when I am sure there was a hesitancy on our part. He might have achieved this in spite of us rather than because of us."

Abbott was well aware that, had he been born with two hands, his pitching alone would not have drawn the same attention to him, nor would it have garnered the overwhelming honors and awards. But he continued to think of himself as just an ordinary person working hard to try to become a good pitcher.

"I don't want kids to be like me because I have one hand," he said. "I want kids to be like Jim Abbott because he is a pitcher at Michigan, and he won the Big 10 championship game, not because he can field a bunt and throw to first."

Resigned to the fact that the publicity would not abate as long as he pitched, Abbott was determined not to let it get to him or change him. A communications major with a B average, he fell behind in his class work but caught up by the time finals came around.

When the 1988 season began, it took Abbott a few weeks to shake the banquet circuit—with its evenings of elaborate dinners and acclaim—out of his system. Texas hammered him for seven runs in his first start, which was broadcast on the sports channel ESPN.

By the middle of May 1988, Abbott had a 9-3 record and was attracting a growing army of scouts to every game. Still the questions about his fielding persisted, no matter how many times he made the plays. Some scouts predicted that he would have to modify the way he kicked his right leg high in the air before throwing a pitch, to curtail base stealers. Scouts for National League teams, whose pitchers have to take their turn at bat, wondered about his ability to swing a bat. College teams use the designated hitter. They also use aluminum bats, which send a ball farther on contact than the wood bats used in professional leagues.

Realizing Abbott's batting ability could affect his chances of being drafted by a National League team, coach Bud Middaugh put Abbott in the lineup as designated hitter in a game against Grand Valley State on March 22. Resting the bat handle on his right arm and grasping both arm and bat in his left, Abbott was 2 for 2. It was the only game in which he batted all year.

One aspect no one seemed concerned about was Abbott's capability to handle the major league media crush. Many a young player has found it easier to cope with major league hitters and pitchers than with major league publicity. Abbott's graciousness and patience under the attacks of reporters with pads and microphones and the television lights and cameras did not go unobserved by the scouts.

One day, California Angels scouting director Bob Fontaine went to the bull pen to watch Abbott throw. It seemed to him that every time Jim turned around there was a camera in his face. Fontaine went away convinced that Abbott had what it took to survive in the big leagues.

Half of Abbott's 16 starts were complete games in the short college season of 1988, but his control was erratic and he was dissatisfied with the high number of walks and hits he gave up. The Wolverines fell short of a third straight Big Ten title, and they never made it to the College World Series while Abbott played on the team.

From the start of his college career, the California Angels in the American League had been the most avid and unwavering believers in Abbott's major league potential. Seven Angels scouts watched him pitch and were impressed with the way he seemed to know how to pitch, not just how to throw hard.

Abbott, who had decided not to enter his senior year at Michigan but to turn pro instead, expected to be picked in the first round of the draft, so it did not surprise him when a reporter called him at home just after noon on June 1, 1988, and told him the Angels had drafted him. It did surprise him when the phone kept ringing for two days as the media built up the story. Jim headed north and went fishing to get away from it all.

The Angels offered Abbott a $200,000 contract, and he did not turn it down. He left the University of Michigan with 84 credits toward his degree. Mike Abbott later commented on his son's having left college before earning a B.A. degree, "His mother will strangle him if he doesn't finish and get his degree some way."

Abbott's dream of a shot at the major leagues was about to come true, but once again it had to be put on hold while he fulfilled another aspiration—representing the United States in the 1988 Olympics in Seoul, South Korea.

Soon after the draft, Abbott headed for the U.S. Olympic team's camp at an old naval base in Millington, Tennessee. The coach, Mark Marquess of Stanford University, drilled them four hours a day without letup. It was hot, and there was not much else to do but work. Restricted to the base, the teammates stayed in the barracks and got to know one another. Abbott was just one of many college stars who had been first-round draft choices or would be the following year. Other players who were drafted were pitchers Andy Benes (San Diego Padres) and Ben McDonald (Baltimore Orioles); infielders Robin Ventura (Chicago White Sox), Mickey Morandini (Philadelphia Phillies), Tino Martinez (Seattle Mariners), and Ty Griffin (Chicago Cubs); and outfielder Ted Wood (San Francisco Giants).

As usual, Abbott drew most of the media attention. The players, too, were caught up in the curiosity; most had never seen him pitch. "The first time you see him," recalled Robin Ventura, "you get caught up in the glove exchange and just how amazing that really is. That overshadowed his pitching at first."

By the time they left camp to begin a three-month, 30,000-mile trek of practice games, Abbott was everybody's friend. The players made 27 stops as they toured across the United States, playing teams from Cuba to Japan and participating in the world tournament in Italy. After 5:00 A.M. flights and four-hour bus rides, the players decided that life in the minor leagues would be a cinch by comparison. The frequent time changes, lack of sleep, strange foods, and long rides wore them down more than the teams they played.

Twice the U.S. team spent two weeks in Japan, where the pitcher's mounds were flat in most ballparks and there was no grass on the infields. Most of the players did not care for sushi, and the beef was served almost raw, but they found a McDonald's and regularly ate there. The pitchers had to face 30-year-old veterans on the national teams wielding aluminum bats. "It was fearsome," Ben McDonald recalled.

They traveled to Parma, Italy, for the World Baseball Tournament and met the Cuban team in the finals. Abbott took a 3–1 lead into the ninth, but a bad call by the umpire at first base went against them, and the Cubans rallied to pull out the victory and retain their world title.

The weary Americans left Parma in the middle of the night by bus, riding six hours to Rome, where they boarded a plane to New Delhi, India. After a few hours waiting there, they took a flight to Tokyo, transferred to a flight to Osaka, and then got on a bus for two-hour ride to Kobe. The journey lasted a total of 30 hours.

Abbott's Olympic teammates had long since forgotten about his one-handedness, but it was new to the Japanese, who were fascinated by Abbott. Arriving in Tokyo, he had disembarked from the plane and found about 100 cameramen waiting for him. Flashbulbs popped and cameras clicked constantly. All the questioning Abbott had put up

Abbott, who celebrated his 21st birthday while in Seoul, South Korea, received daily media coverage during the Olympics; his teammates respected his finesse in handling reporters and learned how to deal with the press by observing Abbott's commendable conduct.

with over the years—first in Flint, then at Michigan, and finally at the Pan-American Games—had begun to ebb. Now it flared up with unprecedented intensity. Every day the team practiced in Japan, whenever Abbott fielded a ground ball or a bunt, the sound of clicking and whirring cameras could be heard. "When I'd field the ball and switch the glove, they'd go bananas," Abbott said. "They think it's a big deal." One day a woman approached him and handed him a scrapbook. In it, there was a frame-by-frame display of Abbott manipulating his glove to make a play.

In addition to the daily media coverage he received, Abbott was asked by some television officials to make a commercial against drugs. The other players did not resent the attention he got; they were just as happy to escape it, and they even kidded Abbott about it. "I learned about dealing with the media from watching Jim," Ben McDonald said, "and it helped me the next year when I had to do it after signing with the Orioles."

When Abbott pitched five shutout innings against a Japanese all-star team, he drew oohs and aahs of wonderment and admiration from the crowd for his dexterity with the glove as well as for his fastball.

The U.S. Olympic team arrived at Olympic Village in Seoul, South Korea, in time to celebrate Abbott's 21st birthday with a 5–3 win over South Korea in the first round. Almost 10,000 athletes from all over the world gathered in the compound. It was as exciting to Abbott to meet American stars of other sports as it was for them to meet him. He was surprised at how many of them were aware of his achievements and at how South Korean children headed straight for him with their autograph books.

Abbott felt a swell of pride when the U.S. flag went up at the start of a game and the national anthem sounded. "You're pitching for U.S.A. and that means something," he said. "It made me hold that hat against my heart a little tighter."

In Olympic competition, once a team qualifies for the final four, the only thing that counts is a victory in the final game. The record during the rest of the games means nothing. Once the United States clinched a semifinal spot, coach Marquess wanted his best pitcher ready to start the gold-medal game, if they got that far. That is why he let Abbott start against Canada on September 23, but pulled him out after just three innings. The other pitchers could not hold the Canadians, who won, 8 to 7.

Three days later, Ben McDonald pitched his second complete game, defeating Puerto Rico, 7 to 2, to put the United States into the gold-medal game against the defending champion, Japan. (Cuba had boycotted the 1988 Olympics for political reasons.)

On September 28, Abbott started the game for the gold medal and took a 4–1 lead on the strength of a home run and single by Tino Martinez, but in the sixth inning he ran into trouble. He began to overthrow, trying to blow the ball past the hitters, and lost his rhythm and control. He walked a batter with the bases loaded, forcing in a run. The catcher, Doug Robbins, looked over to the dugout after every pitch, shaking his head. Andy Benes was warming up in the bull pen. Coach Marquess called time and walked out to the mound. The infielders gathered at the mound.

"We had some good guys in the bull pen," Robin Ventura said, "but Jim was definitely our best pitcher. Everybody knew he could reach back and throw that good pitch when he needed to get the tough out. So we kind of talked the coach into leaving him in."

Another run scored on a ground out and it was 4 to 3 before Abbott got out of the inning. In the top of the eighth, Abbott relaxed a little after Tino Martinez hit his second home run of the game, giving them a two-run lead. The Japanese seldom hit the long ball, and a two-run margin made a possible bloop hit less dangerous. But in the last of the eighth, Abbott gave up a leadoff single, and Benes

Abbott fields a grounder and looks to throw to second base in the fourth inning of the game for the Olympic gold medal on September 28, 1988. The American team defeated the Japanese team, 5 to 3.

was up again in the bull pen. The next batter hit a sharp one-hopper up the middle. It came at him so fast, Abbott barely got the glove back on his left hand when the ball reached him. Thinking double play, Abbott hurriedly grabbed the ball, but it bounced off his glove and rolled away. Abbott discarded the glove as he pounced on the ball, picked it up and, while falling, threw underhand to first base for the putout. His completion of the play despite his bobble evoked a roar of admiration from the crowd that was echoed a few minutes later after two more ground balls ended the threat.

In the ninth inning, all three Japanese batters went down on grounders to third baseman Robin Ventura. When the last out was made, Abbott leaped for joy. The United States had won the gold medal. Abbott's teammates surrounded him and pushed and hugged and tugged at each other until they all went down in a pile of tangled limbs on the mound. Abbott wound up on the bottom of the heap with his nose ground into the dirt, while outfielder Mike Fiore planted a U.S. flag on the mound.

While the rest of the team took a victory lap around the field, Abbott stood on the mound, shaking hands with the Japanese players and savoring the moment. An ultimate victory had eluded him in the Connie Mack League, in high school, and in college. For the first time, he tasted a championship. "It was an incredible feeling when they hung the gold medal around my neck. I think there's something extra about winning a gold in a team sport. We each can say to 19 other guys, 'Hey, we did it.'"

Back in Flint, the Abbotts had stayed up until 3:00 A.M. hoping to see the results, but it was not until they woke again at 7:00 A.M. and watched the game highlights that they were aware of Jim's triumph. Following a 20-hour flight from Seoul, Abbott arrived the following night in Detroit, where his family, hordes of autograph seekers, and the press and TV crews greeted him. He jumped a row of seats to hug his parents, his brother, Chad, and grandparents, Fran and Frank Adams. Then he had to answer the questions.

Wearing his medal around his neck beneath the blue Olympic jacket, Abbott declared, "Winning a gold medal is everything it's cracked up to be, a thrill of a lifetime."

About 500 cheering fans met the Abbotts when they arrived at the Water Street Pavilion in Flint just after 11:00 P.M. After the local politicians had their say, Abbott took a shot at *Money Magazine,* which had recently named Flint as the worst of the nation's 300 largest cities in which to live: "All I know is I loved growing up here and playing sports. If they think Flint is the worst, then every place else must be really wonderful."

Then Jim Abbott headed for Angelo's, for a cheeseburger, and for gravy-laden fries.

Angels pitcher Jim Abbott transfers the ball from his glove to his left hand as he gets ready to pitch against the New York Yankees in May 1989. Abbott went 5 $^{1}/_{3}$ innings against the Yankees that day.

5

MAKING THE TEAM

THERE WERE SOME PRECEDENTS that Jim Abbott could look to for assurance that his goal of pitching in the big leagues was not an impossible dream. In fact, a one-handed pitcher had once thrown a no-hitter in the National League. As a youngster, Hugh Daily had lost his left hand in a gun accident. On September 13, 1883, Daily pitched a 1–0 no-hitter for the Cleveland Spiders. He later pitched two straight one-hitters and struck out 19 in one game. In those days, fielders wore no gloves, so Daily did not have to deal with a mitt.

One Hall of Fame pitcher not only overcame a physical handicap, but he used it to his advantage. When Mordecai Brown was 7, he was operating a corn grinder on his uncle's farm in Indiana. His right hand got caught in the grinder and was mutilated. The accident left him with no forefinger, a crooked middle finger, and a stub of a little finger. He went to work in a coal mine but never gave up his dream of becoming

Mordecai "Three-Fingered" Brown, whose right hand had been injured in a childhood accident, pitched for the Chicago Cubs for eight years. Brown's disfigured hand gave the ball an unusual spin when he pitched, and in 1908, he became the first pitcher to hurl four consecutive shutouts.

a pitcher. One day he discovered that throwing with his mangled hand gave the ball an unusual spin that caused it to move in unexpected ways. "Three-Fingered" Brown, who pitched for the Chicago Cubs from 1904 to 1912, won 20 or more games for the Cubs six years in a row, and 5 World Series games. He was also one of the best fielding pitchers in the league at the time.

Brown's catcher, Jimmy Archer, had a crooked right arm as a result of an injury he received when his arm was burned by hot tar. When the muscles healed, they had shortened and twisted. Archer, however, became the strongest-throwing catcher in the league.

Another three-fingered pitcher, Floyd Newkirk, pitched a no-hitter in the minor leagues and made it to the New York Yankees, where he appeared in only one game in 1934.

Other pitchers who refused to give in to adversity include Leavitt "Buddy" Daley, a natural right-hander whose right arm was crippled by polio and who learned to throw left-handed to become an American League All-Star pitcher in 1959 and 1960; Walter "Lefty" Stewart, who learned to pitch left-handed after he lost a finger on his right hand and went on to win 100 games in the big leagues from 1921 to 1935; Tom "Lefty" Sunkel, who pitched for three years after losing the sight in his left eye in 1941; Claude Jonnard, who made it to the majors despite being blind in one eye, and pitched from 1921 to 1929; and Luther "Dummy" Taylor, a deaf-mute star pitcher for the champion New York Giants in the early 1900s.

Perhaps the greatest success of any handicapped player was that of William "Dummy" Hoy, a deaf-mute outfielder who made more than 2,000 hits in his 14-year career, mostly in the 19th century.

Abbott once saw a movie about Monty Stratton, a big league pitcher during the 1930s who lost a leg in a hunting accident and pitched for several years in the minor leagues afterward. But the example most often cited to Abbott was that of Pete Gray. Like Abbott, Gray always wanted to be a ballplayer. When he was six, his right arm was crushed under the wheel of a truck, leaving him with just a stump below his right shoulder. A natural right-hander, Gray learned to throw and bat with his left arm. He threw rocks in the air and hit them. He was also a very fast runner. An outfielder, he rolled the ball across his chest after he caught it, stuck the glove under his stump, grabbed the ball, and threw it, seemingly all in one motion.

Pete Gray made it to the minor leagues, where he batted .333 for Memphis in 1944. He hit 5 home runs and stole 68 bases and won the Southern Association's Most Valuable Player Award. The player shortage caused by World War II earned him a chance to play in the major leagues. In 1945, he batted .218 for the St. Louis Browns in the American League. The following year, the war ended and Pete Gray went back to the minors. But he had proved that a one-armed player could make it to the big leagues.

Pete Gray's example was not dismissed by Jim Abbott, but Gray was not Abbott's inspiration. For Abbott never thought of himself as a one-armed ballplayer. He was a pitcher and as such he looked up to Nolan Ryan and Orel Hershiser. "I didn't grow up saying, 'I want to be the next Pete Gray.' The only goal I had in mind was to be the next Nolan Ryan."

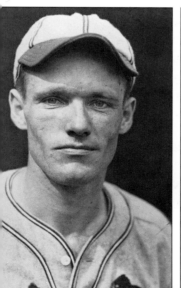

Tom "Lefty" Sunkel (left) pitched for the St. Louis Cardinals before he became blind in his left eye. He went on to pitch for the New York Giants and the Brooklyn Dodgers. Leavitt "Buddy" Daley's (right) right arm was crippled by polio; however, Daley learned to pitch with his left hand and became an American League All-Star pitcher in 1959 and 1960.

Pete Gray, who lost his right arm at the age of six, learned to throw and bat with his left arm. Gray played in the minor leagues, and during World War II, he became an outfielder for the St. Louis Browns.

When Abbott reported to Gene Autry Field in Mesa, Arizona, for the start of the California Angels' spring training on March 1, 1989, he went from being the ace of the U.S. Olympic team to one among many rookie prospects. The thrills and excitement of the gold-medal victory in South Korea gave way to a sense of wonder and awe the first time he put on a major league uniform.

"I couldn't believe it," he said. "Lance Parrish . . . Dan Petry, my idol when I was a high school pitcher. . . . Here I am in the same clubhouse with these guys, putting on my red shoes and my uniform."

Abbott hoped to keep a low profile. "I'm just a rookie. I don't want to step on anyone's toes." But that was not possible. The number 60 he wore on his shirt did not make him indistinguishable from the other high-numbered newcomers sprinting in the outfield. As he had discovered in Japan, wherever he went, there were new reporters who had never had a chance to ask him the questions he had heard a hundred times before.

It was easy to spot him: just look for the largest group of people not in uniform. Reporters from newspapers, magazines, radio, and television swarmed around him. His answers were almost automatic: "My parents never said I couldn't do this or that. A few people tried to tell me I wouldn't go far in sports but I didn't listen to them. I always thought I would play pro ball."

Cameramen waited for a bunt or ground ball to be hit back to Abbott to record it on film; invariably he made the ordinary plays routinely, just like any other pitcher.

A writer for Abbott's hometown newspaper, the *Flint Journal,* traveled to Mesa to interview him. "There is a different line of questioning and a different approach by both player and media," Abbott told him. "It may sound harsh, but it is kind of an antagonistic approach at the pro level. . . . I feel more like public property. I think it takes its toll. I'm not saying I'm crying out to be heard. I'm something new to a lot of people. I'm also very, very old to a lot of other people."

Tim Mead, the Angels public relations director, asked the media to meet with Jim in formal press conferences, rather than assaulting him one at a time as soon as his workout was completed.

"The kid is not looking for attention," Mead explained, "and we're not trying to isolate him, but the questions have become a little personal. I see frustration."

Mead had deliberately omitted any mention of Abbott's birth defect in the Angels media guide. "There is enough focus on the hand. I'll buy you dinner in Anaheim if you can show me five articles that don't mention it."

Other players felt the effects of Abbott's presence; reporters sought their reactions to his situation. "They asked us if we thought Jim was the real thing [or just a publicity gimmick]," said infielder Mark McLemore. "I wondered, too, until I saw him pitch. Once I saw him getting hitters out, and make the fielding plays, he was just another pitcher to us. Some guys had concerns over whether he could handle the media attention they saw him getting. But he handled it fine."

Veteran outfielder Chili Davis agreed. "Players were curious when they were first going to see him. The first time you saw him flip the glove and make a fielding play, you said, 'Wow, that's amazing.' But after a few times you ignored it. Later, when new players saw it for the first time,

Angels general manager Mike Port (right) and Jim Abbott show Abbott's jersey during Abbott's first press conference, in which he was introduced as a member of the team.

Gene Autry Field in Mesa, Arizona, was the site for the Angels spring training camp when Abbott joined the team in 1989. Today, the Angels train at the Tempe Diablo Complex in Tempe, Arizona.

they went, 'Wow, that's amazing,' but we told them, 'No, it's not; he's always done that.'"

Abbott had signed a minor league contract and expected to start the season with the Class AA farm team at Midland, Texas.

He knew he could not consistently throw his curve ball for strikes, and he would have to develop another pitch to go with his fastball.

In spring practice, the rawest rookie is thrown into action with the oldest veterans. Assigned to throw batting practice soon after he arrived, Abbott stood on the mound nervously. "Just looking around at everything here," he said, "it hits you. A big league camp."

Then he noticed that the catcher behind the plate was Lance Parrish, whom the 12-year-old Jim had admired when Parrish caught for the Detroit Tigers. Abbott stared at the big mitt with the bright orange ring around it. Parrish was staring back at Abbott. "I had never seen anyone with one hand play ball, so it was fascinating to me to watch him and see how he did things. But after the first few days it eased up, and you don't give it a second thought."

The sound of the bat hitting the ball was another new sensation for Abbott. In all of his previous games, teams had used aluminum bats. But in the major leagues they use wooden bats that make a more solid, less pinging sound on contact.

Despite the high marks scouts had given him, Abbott knew that he had a lot to learn. His explosive fastball and his slider, which had been his "out" pitch in the Olympics, would not be enough to win in the majors. "My curve needs work and my change-up definitely needs work," he said.

Abbott also had little experience in holding men on base because so few batters had ever gotten on base against him. He would have to modify his high-kick windup that gave baserunners a big jump.

Jim Abbott, however, had one advantage over other young pitchers, according to former major league manager

Whitey Herzog: "Young pitchers coming out of college have been pitching to guys with aluminum bats, where inside pitches can be hit far, so they are used to pitching everybody away, and when they come up against wooden bats, they are pitching into hitters' strength. Abbott was unusual in that he came up pitching right-handed batters inside. That's why he broke so many bats."

When he read the sports pages, Abbott could not avoid all the ink about himself. As it was throughout his high school and college days, every mention of his name was followed by the phrase "who was born without a right hand," which annoyed him. There was constant speculation about his ability to field his position; somehow, picking up bunts and snaring one-hoppers was supposed to be more difficult in the big leagues.

Abbott's roommate in camp, and for the next few years, was Rick Turner, the bull pen catcher who had never swung a bat in the major leagues. They talked for hours into the night, the catcher whose dreams had never materialized, and the ballyhooed one-handed pitcher who wondered if he would fulfill all the predictions of stardom that others were making for him. Abbott was aware that many highly touted high school and college stars never made it to the top.

One day Abbott messed up a potential double play comebacker failing to get the ball out of his glove in time. But among the Angels coaches, the realization that he was not the best fielding pitcher in camp was tempered by the knowledge that a lot of two-handed pitchers had their problems with the glove, too. In one of the spring drills, the pitchers stood on the mound as coach Deron Johnson flipped a ball on the ground and the pitchers had to pick it up and throw to first. Abbott maneuvered the glove and ball so quickly, nobody could follow how he did it.

Manager Doug Rader and pitching coach Marcel Lachemann preferred to stress Abbott's "good stuff, good delivery," and pitching smarts. They began to think of starting

Pitching coach Marcel Lachemann gives Abbott a few pointers during Abbott's workout. Lachemann had recognized Abbott's "good stuff, good delivery," and pitching smarts during spring training.

Detroit Tigers catcher Lance Parrish tags the Padres' Alan Gibson out at home plate during the 1984 World Series game. Parrish was one of Abbott's idols when Abbott was a youth; he used to focus on Parrish's catcher's mitt with the orange ring on it whenever he attended a Detroit Tigers game. Parrish was playing for the Angels when Abbott became his teammate in 1989.

him at a higher level, in the AAA Pacific Coast League. If he succeeded there and the Angels needed pitching help, perhaps they would bring him up later in the season.

Abbott's first spring start came when the Angels traveled to Yuma, Arizona, for an exhibition game against San Diego. So many reporters covered it that the atmosphere resembled a World Series. Dave Cunningham, who covered the Angels for the *Long Beach Press-Telegram,* was struck by Abbott's "grace under pressure. He was just 22, and very smooth, a class act, fielding the same stupid questions he had heard all his life."

Abbott struck out five and gave up one run in his first innings of work.

On March 7, 1989, Abbott faced the world champion Oakland A's. He had gone to the 1988 World Series and imagined pitching against the A's as he watched the games. "I know it was just an exhibition game," he said, "but I'll be honest, it was a thrill facing José Canseco." He struck out the A's slugger.

Off the field, the demands on Abbott's time never let up. Every day, more than 100 letters arrived for him. The top of his locker in the rookies' corner of the clubhouse was stuffed to overflowing. He could not keep up with all of the fan mail, no matter how conscientious he was in trying to answer all of it.

Parents approached him after practice with their young sons in tow, 9- and 10-year-old boys with one hand or one arm. Some were Little Leaguers. Most were very shy and said little. Abbott always had an encouraging word for each of them.

Abbott's impressive showing and his "grace under pressure" of the media blitz led the Angels to consider his skipping the minor leagues and opening the season in Anaheim. Some critics, however, charged the Angels managers with moving Abbott up too fast just to benefit from the publicity surrounding the novelty of the one-handed pitcher.

The Angels had finished fourth in the American League (AL) West the year before and had lost their last 12 games. They had a mix of veteran and young pitchers, and competition for the fifth starter's slot was keen. They had won the AL West title in 1986 with some of those same pitchers, but they had not been a winning team since. If anyone faltered, there would be an opportunity for someone new to step in. One of the veteran pitchers was Dan Petry, who befriended Abbott in Mesa, passing along his work ethic: do five minutes more work than the next guy. "Avoid highs and lows," he counseled, "and remember, you are only as good as your last outing."

Then a sore shoulder knocked the 30-year-old Petry out of the starting rotation, and Jim Abbott took his place. Abbott wanted to believe it was his ability and not his oddity that earned him the chance.

When the Angels announced that Abbott would open the season with them, bypassing the minors, Abbott received one message that he treasured above all the rest, and it is the only memento of his career displayed in his home: a telegram of congratulations from the one player he most wanted to emulate—pitcher Nolan Ryan.

Although Abbott had been ranked high by scouts, he knew that as a major leaguer he needed to improve his fastball, slider, and curveball.

On August 31, 1989, rookie Abbott stops the Red Sox, 4 to 0, ending their nine-game winning streak. After the Angels won the game, Abbott was given a standing ovation at Boston's Fenway Park.

6

FULFILLING A DREAM

ANAHEIM, CALIFORNIA, was a world apart from Flint, Michigan. Abbott was not used to the traffic congestion, the enormous numbers of people, and the many different lifestyles. Nevertheless, he adapted to it and enjoyed the nearby beaches and mountains more than his parents thought he would. "They were worried how I was going to handle living in California. They were afraid I was going to flip out."

Larger numbers of people in Anaheim, of course, meant there would be more fans of Abbott. It was impossible for him to go shopping or walk around at a mall without being recognized. He found more anonymity in Las Vegas, Nevada, a few hours away, where people were too preoccupied with gambling to give him more than a quick nod of recognition.

As soon as Abbott made the team, the Angels were flooded with requests from more than 100 charities and organizations, all wanting a piece of his time. Abbott had enough to deal with in trying to establish himself as a big league pitcher. Like any rookie, he needed time to get acclimated to the major leagues, to learn his way around, to become acquainted with his teammates, and to settle in. "The other things that people are asking of me don't have anything to do with baseball," he said. "I don't know if that's always fair to ask of me."

Lance Parrish observed, "His rookie year was one of the most difficult things I've ever seen anyone go through. Everywhere he went, everybody wanted to talk to him. I don't know how he did as well as he did on the field. It amazed me how he could keep his composure and be so gracious."

Occasionally it did get to him, as it would to anyone. "You're trying to get acquainted with a new team, and there's constantly someone with a camera in your face, telling you you're different. . . . I'd rather be left alone," Abbott admitted.

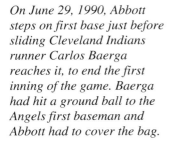

On June 29, 1990, Abbott steps on first base just before sliding Cleveland Indians runner Carlos Baerga reaches it, to end the first inning of the game. Baerga had hit a ground ball to the Angels first baseman and Abbott had to cover the bag.

But being left alone was not in the cards for Jim Abbott. The American League considered Jim a special case, too, but they made no exceptions in the rules for him. However, league president Dr. Bobby Brown did give the umpires some leeway in interpreting the rules. At the start of the season, Dr. Brown issued the following order: "Pitcher Jim Abbott . . . has only one hand (left). When he is in the set position, he rotates and fixes the ball in his hand prior to pitching. He will be allowed to do this without penalty." If another pitcher tried this maneuver, he could be called for a balk (an illegal motion while the pitcher is in position).

Umpires also faced another tricky predicament: what if Abbott accidentally dropped his glove while fielding a ball? It is against the rules to throw a glove at a batted ball. Nonetheless, most umpires felt they would give Abbott the benefit of the doubt if such a situation ever occurred.

When Abbott warmed up to start his first big league game on April 8, 1989, against Seattle, he considered himself fortunate to have survived all the obstacles that he had hurdled to reach his goal. "My dad thinks that I have been chosen," he said. "He thinks there is a reason for all this to happen."

In spite of this, Abbott lost his first start, 7 to 0.

Five days later he lost again, 5 to 0, to Oakland. A pattern had begun that would plague Abbott for the first four years of his career. He had more trouble with his own team's batters than the ones he pitched against, for they scored very few runs whenever he was on the mound. But, as his teammate and fellow southpaw Chuck Finley pointed out, "Lack of support is something you deal with. When you come to the big leagues you're not guaranteed how long you'll be there or how many runs you'll get or how many games you'll win. You take your chances."

Abbott missed a start when cold weather canceled his April 18 turn in Chicago, and he had to endure 10 days of inactivity.

"I felt like I was just along for the ride," he said. "I didn't feel like I was earning my keep, that I was contributing."

Players and pitchers have always joshed each other about who has the easier job. Hitters say that starting pitchers have to work only once every five or six days. Pitchers reply that a hitter who goes hitless one night has a chance to come back the next day and do better, but a pitcher who gets roughed up in a game has four or five days to brood about it before he can make amends.

Abbott's next chance to start came on April 24 against Baltimore at home. He struggled through six innings, once walking three in a row, before leaving with a 3–2 lead. It was up to relievers Greg Minton and Bryan Harvey to save the game for him. While icing down his shoulder in the clubhouse, Abbott listened nervously to the radio as the Orioles got three men on base and two outs in the eighth. He held his breath as the count reached 3 and 1 on the next batter, then sighed with relief as the hitter struck out. The Orioles went down in the ninth, and an elated Abbott had that elusive first win in the books.

By the time he beat Toronto to even his record at 2-2, opposing players began to shift their focus from Abbott's so-called handicap to his pitching. They remained awed by what he had accomplished. "If you haven't been doing it all your life," said Nolan Ryan, "it's impossible to comprehend." They now realized they were up against a lefty who knew what he was doing on the mound.

"He was a lot of fun to catch," Parrish said. "When he was on he could breeze through a game. You got the feeling that he was in control. Like Steve Carlton, Jim had an even demeanor on the mound, no matter the score or situation. Jim might slam his glove in disgust in the dugout or run down the ramp to the clubhouse yelling and screaming but he showed nothing on the mound."

Abbott had plenty to get upset about, even if he did not show it. Not only did his team score very few runs for him, but he probably led the league in cheap hits. "I don't know how many games I caught him in which guys would bloop a hit just over the infield or beat out a little bleeder after he made a perfect pitch to jam them," Parrish recalled. "He made a lot of out pitches that wound up as cheap hits that killed him. I would say to myself, 'It isn't fair.'"

Abbott's fastball was a natural cut fastball, cutting inside to a right-handed batter at the last instant, causing a lot of broken bats. "A cut fastball breaks less than a curve or slider, but more than a fastball," Angels outfielder Dave Winfield explained. "For a left-hander to get that in on the hands of a right-handed batter doesn't happen that frequently. The speed of the pitch can lull a batter into getting jammed. If he can throw it like a regular fastball so you don't think it's in on your hands, and bam—it's there—your bat's gone; he's made a lamp out of your bat."

Abbott had a hard time throwing the ball straight when he wanted to, or inside to left-handed swingers. As a result, he fared better against right-handers. Some switch-hitters found it easier to hit against him from the left side of the plate. "When we tried to get him to work the other side of the plate, he had a lot of trouble hitting the outside corner to a right-hander," Parrish said. "For a while guys just looked inside on him because they knew that was where they would get it. At this level you can't get away with throwing one pitch in the same spot all the time. His cut fastball thrown on the outside wound up cutting right over the plate, and that is trouble. He had a lot of problems his first year throwing that fastball outside. It would go way up or way out."

When Abbott had pitched in the Pan-American Games, some players with professional experience had told him, "If you're a decent pitcher, the majors will force you to become a better pitcher." They meant that better hitters would force him to improve his own game in order to beat them.

Abbott worked on his curve and change-up. Being able to change speeds is important to a winning pitcher, but it did not come easily to Abbott. He threw only one change-up all year and it was not a good one, and he did not have the confidence to try it again.

When the Angels played Detroit on May 3, Abbott stayed at home in Flint. As a visitor, he was relieved of doing any chores around the house. He and Mike Staisil hit Angelo's a few times, driving by Kearsley Park on the way, where Jim had first learned to pitch.

It was a strange experience for him to drive to Tiger Stadium and park his Jeep in the players' lot, walk into the visiting team's clubhouse, and see the ancient stadium from the player's perspective. "It was weird, smaller from the field than it had looked from the seats," he reflected. He found himself still rooting for the Tigers, as long as they were in the other division, but he intended to go all out to beat them. But he had to wait for that opportunity; it rained on the day he was scheduled to pitch.

Abbott brought with him to the big leagues the same spirited, rah-rah, jazz-it-up attitude he had displayed since

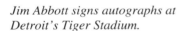

Jim Abbott signs autographs at Detroit's Tiger Stadium.

his Little League days. All through high school and college he had been an enthusiastic cheerleader on the bench. Big league dugouts, however, are usually as silent as a tomb, and Abbott took some kidding because of his college spirit. When he got pumped up, he would slap his hand in his glove and raise his arms as if to say, "Yeah, way to go," while the other players eyed him with amusement. Once, during a game, a fight started in the stands and he jumped up, yelling, "Fight, fight." When nobody else shared his excitement, his face reddened, and he sat down quietly.

Abbott was dismayed by the lack of pep and the apparently individual approach taken by the established stars. He and his roommate, bull pen catcher Rick Turner, discussed it. "You find there are individuals who are not concerned with the team effort, but are more concerned with putting up numbers to receive more money," Turner said. "That really upset [Abbott] and initially was a surprise to him. . . . An individual is concerned more about his personal statistics rather than laying down a bunt, getting a guy over, that sort of thing, because you don't get any money in arbitration for those things."

Although he was now a big leaguer himself, Abbott remained an eager autograph collector. He asked older players he met around the league to sign balls, which he sent to his brother, Chad, who was preparing to attend the University of Michigan to study zoology. One day, Lou Brock, Ernie Banks, and other National League stars whom Abbott had read about or seen on television came to Anaheim for an old-timers game. Abbott wanted to get a ball signed by Brock, but he hesitated to approach him. In the Angels clubhouse, someone came up to Abbott and told him that Lou Brock wanted to meet him. "He wants to meet *me*?" Abbott asked in amazement. He got the ball signed by Brock, and it is one of his most-prized possessions.

Wherever he went, Abbott attracted hordes of young people with cards, balls, and scraps of paper to be signed.

Abbott acknowledges a standing ovation given by the fans at Yankee Stadium after he pitched six innings. Abbott allowed 10 hits but only three batters scored, and the Angels defeated the Yankees, 11 to 4.

Abbott has high esteem for Lou Brock, who was inducted into the Baseball Hall of Fame in 1985. When Abbott became a major leaguer, he hoped to get an autographed baseball from Brock but was timid about approaching the all-time leader in stolen bases. Brock, himself, admired Abbott and wanted to meet the rookie pitcher when Brock was in Anaheim for an old-timers game.

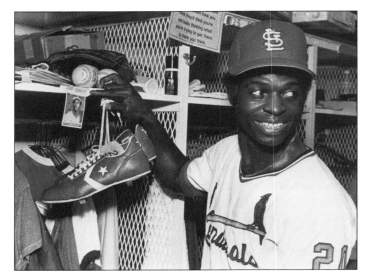

When he looked down at a young autograph seeker, he saw himself, years earlier, standing outside Tiger Stadium while his yawning father waited patiently for him. Although he enjoyed the attention, the demands could be crushing at times, and the grudge he had carried against Jim Rice for once rudely rebuffing him dissolved to the point where he wanted "to go up to Rice and apologize."

In Anaheim, Abbott discovered a secret exit behind the right field wall where a friend could wait in his car after games. Otherwise Abbott would be mobbed and it would be hours before he could get away. Rick Turner recalled coming out of the Kingdome in Seattle one night after a game. "The bus had already gone to the hotel and he got mobbed by hundreds of autograph seekers, kids and adults. It took all our efforts to get through it to a cab. It was amazing to me, but he never complained."

Whenever the Angels faced an opposing team for the first time, the players stared in disbelief as Abbott practiced or warmed up. After they batted against him, the fascination wore off and he became just another pitcher to them. In each city in which he played, there were still reporters who asked all of the old questions.

"Abbie is a wonderful man," said Angels manager Doug Rader, "a tremendous human being in every way. He's patient, very mature. . . . To be able to deal with the constant attention the way he has, it's absolutely amazing to me."

Abbott was uneasy with being cast as a role model, an idol for the physically challenged. But he realized that people saw him that way, and he did not wish to duck the responsibility that went with his visible position. Whenever he saw a child with one hand or some other disability, he could not turn away without responding. Abbott explained:

> I saw so much of it during the season, kids in every city. You can't grow hardened to it, the awareness of what that kid and his parents will go through.
>
> I had it easy, with supportive parents. But it won't always be that way, and any support you can give will have an amazing effect. Those are the things I had to take into account, when I was a bit tired, when all I wanted to do was lie on a bed.

One day a boy came into the clubhouse with his parents. He had only parts of two fingers on one hand. He asked Abbott if kids had been mean to him when he was growing up, adding that he had been called "crab" at camp. "Yeah," Abbott said, "they used to say my hand looked like a foot. Do you think teasing is a problem?"

"No," the youngster replied.

"Is there anything you can't do?" Abbott asked.

"No."

"Well, I don't think so either." Abbott looked around the room and said, "Look, I'm playing with guys like Dave Winfield, Wally Joyner, and Dave Parker. I'm playing with them, and I'm just like you."

Later Abbott told a writer, "I'd never said that before, that I was thrilled to be here and it didn't matter if I had two good hands. But I put myself in that kid's shoes and

Abbott bats in the second inning of a game against the Los Angeles Dodgers in April 1990. He made it safely to first base after bunting the ball. Angels manager Doug Rader once said of Abbott, "Abbie is a wonderful man . . . a tremendous human being in every way."

remembered what I was like at his age. I'm sure that kids need someone to relate to, but so do their parents. Most of the time I think it's my parents these people should be talking to, not me."

The number of people who could meet him was multiplied by a thousand who could not, and those people wrote letters to him instead. Abbott tried to answer them all, knowing the entire time that the answer lay not in everyone's trying to emulate him, but in their finding the strength and motivation within themselves that he had found and relied upon.

Two days after Abbott had won his first major league game, he wrote to a little girl who had lost a hand in an accident: "As your parents probably told you, I was born without a right hand. That automatically made me different from other kids around. But know what? It made me different only in their eyes. I figured this was what the Good Lord wanted me to work with so it was my responsibility to become as good as I could at whatever I chose to do, regardless of my handicap."

But even Abbott got upset with phone calls he received at dawn from people wanting something from him. "It's nice to have that kind of following, but too much of a good thing can be a burden. You try to be everything to everybody and you end up losing yourself. You need time to get away from it."

Abbott's roommate on the road, Rick Turner, felt the brunt of it, too. "There comes a time when you have to draw the line," Turner said. "We could shut the phone off in the hotels, but then your friends and family can't get through to you. I had to watch myself, because there were times I was ready to get mad about the phone calls, and I had to be careful because he had so many friends from his hometown, high school and college and the Olympics, and he kept in touch with them. So you couldn't just pick up the phone and be upset because somebody called and it was late."

While attending the dedication of the Jim Abbott Adaptive Playfield at the Little Village School, a school for children with developmental disabilities in Garden City, New York, Abbott (center) poses with students Colin Ryan (right) and Michael Bauer. Abbott encourages children with disabilities to find their own strengths and motivation to accomplish all that they yearn to do.

Ballplayers often tease and razz each other, usually picking on some outstanding physical feature, a habit, or some superstition. Sometimes the riding can be cruel. For example, one player took a tasteless shot at Abbott's lack of a hand, and it fell flat. "Most guys had good taste and there really was not a whole lot of that," Turner recalled. "Jim and I talked about it, and his attitude was, 'It's easy to go for the jugular, the obvious. Be creative, come up with something genuinely funny and not obvious about me.'"

Abbott did not mind the good-natured ribbing that everyone took—pitcher Kirk McCaskill did not let Abbott forget: "I can kick his butt in basketball"—and he readily dished it out himself.

Whatever activity anyone wanted to do on a day off— golf, fish, swim, or roughhouse—Abbott was right there, ready to participate. In friendly wrestling and boxing matches, his stump, according to his teammates, is as hard as the bottom of a ketchup bottle and makes an effective weapon. "No, no," the other guys would yell, "don't stump me."

One of baseball's traditional pranks is the hotfoot. Some players have been known to crawl the length of the dugout, under the bench, and behind the unsuspecting player's legs, just to light up a shoelace. Among the Angels, pitcher Bert Blyleven was the chief shoe arsonist. When executed perfectly, it does not take long for the shoe tongue to catch fire and for flames to start licking up the startled player's leg.

Abbott managed to avoid his baptism by fire for about a month. He was standing while talking to a gathering of reporters in the dugout before a game when Blyleven shouted, "Hey, Abbott, did your house burn down?" Just then a strong odor filled the air. Using a foot-long lighter, Blyleven had set Abbott's shoestring ablaze. Abbott calmly put the fire out and continued to answer questions.

"That's my first one," he said. But it was a measure of acceptance. He was one of the guys now, nothing special, and that was the way he wanted it.

Lasting only three innings in a 5–2 loss to New York, Abbott was determined to prove to himself that he was not that bad a pitcher. In his next start, on May 17, 1989, he turned in his first shutout, a 4-hitter to beat Roger Clemens and the Boston Red Sox, 5 to 0.

Abbott was not intimidated by big league hitters. The strike zone belonged to him. If they crowded the plate on him, he did not hesitate to fire his fastball inside to drive them back. One night in June, Milwaukee's Gus Polidor leaned over the plate to put down a bunt. Abbott's fastball hit him in the chest. Polidor ran at Abbott; both teams raced onto the field, but, as usual, nothing happened except some pushing and jawing. The next batter bunted, but Abbott fielded it cleanly.

Still, Abbott could not be certain that he was being accepted by the fans as just another pitcher. When he left that game after pitching seven shutout innings, the crowd gave him a standing ovation. "As much as you appreciate it," he said, "you wonder whether it's because they just feel sorry for you."

When the Angels returned to Detroit, Abbott started for the first time at Tiger Stadium on Saturday, June 17, 1989.

With his family, friends, former coaches, and high school buddies watching, Abbott could feel the emotional tide rising as he warmed up. He did not settle down until a three-run homer in the first inning erased his jitters and brought him back to reality. He pitched out of trouble in the second inning and was in control from then on, winning 6 to 3. Dan Petry helped to finish the game.

Throughout the season, Abbott stayed around .500. On July 29, he beat the White Sox, 8 to 5, at home. (He would not win another home game until almost a year later, on July 14, 1990, after 12 winless starts.) He won his 10th game on August 6, 1989, 6 to 0, over the Milwaukee Brewers and blanked the Boston Red Sox again at Fenway Park on August 30.

Abbott finished 1989 with 12 wins and 12 losses and a 3.92 ERA. In his 12 losses the Angels averaged under two runs a game. Some games in which he left with a lead were later lost by poor relief pitching. In the field he made just three errors.

During the winter, Abbott visited Flint and Ann Arbor and returned to Japan in December to film a television commercial, work in a charity drive, and help at a baseball clinic. Back in Anaheim, he played golf and worked on his curveball. During this time, Abbott's likeness appeared among a set of baseball stamps released by St. Vincent Island in the West Indies.

With that first year behind him, Abbott had fulfilled his early dream of reaching the big leagues. He had become accepted for what he was by other players—an excellent left-handed pitcher with unlimited potential. But it seemed that every time one dream came true, another took its place. As Abbott told a reporter, he now dreamed of "waking up in the morning, getting the paper and reading a whole story about a game I pitched, with no reference to the fact that I was born with one hand."

Abbott worked with pitching coach Marcel Lachemann to improve his change-up and to shorten his stride while delivering a pitch. He learned that the key to confounding a baserunner is in holding the ball varying lengths of time before pitching it.

7

A PITCHER'S LIFE

JIM ABBOTT WENT into spring training in 1990 determined to pursue a nice, quiet career. He set two goals for himself: to win 15 games and to rid himself of the disappointment he felt when the Angels renewed his contract for $185,000. It was not the amount that upset him so much as the disparity between his pay and that of some of his peers whose performances had been no better than his. But he did not make a big public issue of it. "The last thing people want to hear is somebody complaining about their salary when some guy had to work in an auto shop in Flint seven days a week," he said.

Although the media attention lessened from the year before, Abbott still attracted more of the curious and admiring fans than any other player, and nobody envied him for it.

Working with pitching coach Marcel Lachemann, Abbott still had a hard time getting the feel of throwing a change-up, which requires the same arm speed and motion as a fastball while taking something off its velocity. He practiced shortening his stride with men on base, sliding his right foot instead of lifting it high before delivering the pitch. He learned that the key to confusing a baserunner is in holding the ball varying lengths of time before throwing it—a second or two longer one time than another—to mess up the runner's timing. The longer the runner is forced to stay in a crouch, the more his legs will tire. This, too, came slowly to Abbott, although he worked at it relentlessly. It would take him a few years to curb base stealers more effectively.

During his rookie year, Abbott had begun to develop a book on the hitters in which he noted the kinds of pitches and locations they liked and did not like, and how to pitch to each batter. Such notations are essential to the success of a pitcher. One of the league's sluggers whom Abbott did not know yet was the Yankees' Dave Winfield, who had missed the 1989 season after a back operation. The first time the two teams met, Winfield sought out Abbott on the field and wished him luck in his career. "You're quite a player," Winfield told him, "and you positively influence a lot of people."

But amazement and admiration were forgotten when Winfield faced Abbott for the first time with a bat in his hands. "I just wanted to do my best to make sure he didn't get me out," Winfield said. "I didn't want a guy with what seemingly looked like a handicap to get me out. And he was a rookie pitcher to me. He hadn't faced me. When a younger player faces a veteran, those are little steps they have to achieve to feel really comfortable and confident in the big leagues. I wasn't going to give him any quarter. I was going to bear down on him."

Later that year, Winfield was traded to the Angels and he actually got to know Abbott. "I like him a lot," he said. "Good head, good heart."

The Angels were a break-even team, finishing fourth, and Abbott paralleled their 1990 season with a 10-14 record. He gave up more hits than anybody else in the league. (He had a 4.51 ERA.) His record might have been better, however, if the Angels had scored more than 15 runs total in his 14 losses.

Abbott's troubles continued in 1991. He lost his first four decisions, not to tough luck, but by giving up an average of six earned runs a game. He began to question if he had what it took to succeed in the major leagues. The press and radio talk shows were filled with speculation about when and whether the Angels should send him down to the minor leagues for more experience. But at least the critics concentrated on his poor pitching; nobody talked about his doing it with only one hand, and that was some consolation to him. "Even though people were saying 'This guy stinks,' it made me think that I've finally arrived," explained Abbott.

Still unable to master the change-up, he had lost confidence in his fastball and slider and tried to change his style by being "cuter," trying to lure the hitters into swinging at pitches a little off the plate instead of challenging them with his best stuff. The strategy did not work.

One day, during an early workout in Minnesota, while Abbott and Rick Turner sat in the bull pen, Turner urged him to forget about how other people pitched and to return to the ways that had gotten him to the big leagues. "Don't be afraid to fail," Turner told Abbott, "but go out swinging if that's what it takes."

Abbott vowed to pitch more aggressively with his 94-MPH cut fastball. On May 5, 1991, he beat the Orioles, 6 to 4, for his first win in nine starts, then racked up a 7-6 record by the midpoint of the season.

In every game he pitched, however, Jim Abbott had two enemies: the batter and himself. A perfectionist and a very intense competitor, he was his own harshest critic. "He expects more out of himself than any pitcher I've ever known," said manager Buck Rodgers, who had replaced Doug Rader on August 26, 1990. "If a guy gets a base hit off him, the guy shouldn't have. If he made a bad pitch, he shouldn't have. Once he was so miffed at himself he threw his glove down on the mound in disgust because he had hung a slider. But to the 40,000 fans in the stands it looked like he was angry with a fielder for not making a play. The next day I took him aside and told him what he had done and how it looked. He didn't realize that it looked like he was showing up his teammates, and was very apologetic."

Like most pitchers, Abbott mulled over his mistakes and losses for days. Once he made a throwing error that cost the Angels a game and he felt that he had let everyone down. After the game, when reporters crowded around him, he sat fuming at himself so much that he would not talk to them at first, and when he did, it was through clenched teeth to hold back his anger.

"It's a very emotional thing to be competitive," Turner said, "to want to perform at your highest level. You are taking a risk, laying a lot on the line, and Jim was well aware of that."

On the field, things happened when Abbott pitched that would have strained anyone's patience. "There were extremely frustrating times," Turner added, "lack of offense or defense, things that don't show on paper, like a guy getting a hit because a fielder lacked the range or proper position to prevent it. The pitcher made a good pitch, got the ground ball, but they didn't make the play. You can sing the blues all you want, but that sort of thing happens all the time." But Abbott never used lack of support for an excuse; he blamed himself for every loss. Nevertheless, the Angels continued to score runs in dribs and drabs. "He felt that he had to pitch a shutout every game," Rodgers said, "and when you do that, you don't allow yourself any margin for error, and you are going to make some. I told him, 'You can't control how many runs we score. All you can control is how many men you allow to get on base. If they get one run and hold us to zero, you can't do a thing about it. So don't try.'"

Abbott may have wished he could swing a bat (in his only major league at-bat, he had hit a triple in a March exhibition game), but the designated hitter batted for the pitcher in the American League.

In the second half of the season, Abbott improved his performance, putting up 11 wins against 5 losses for a final record of 18 and 11. Four times he left with a lead in the seventh or eighth, but the bull pen failed to hold it for him. He resisted coming out of a game, a trait any manager likes to see in a pitcher, and worked 243 innings. His record improved in almost every category. He made only two errors, and his outstanding plays were finally reported with no mention of his missing right hand.

The Angels' three southpaws—Abbott, Chuck Finley, and Mark Langston—combined for 55 of the team's 81 victories in 1991, but they slid to seventh in the AL West. Amid rumors of a trade involving one or more of them, Abbott and closer Bryan Harvey were voted the Angels' most valuable players by their teammates. Abbott placed third in the voting for the Cy Young Award, an honor given annually to the best pitcher in each league.

In addition to his fellow pitchers, Abbott's closest friends remained the guys he had grown up with in Flint. He shared a condominium in Newport Beach, California, with John Lutton, a friend since elementary school. He enjoyed the year-round life at the beach with Rick Turner,

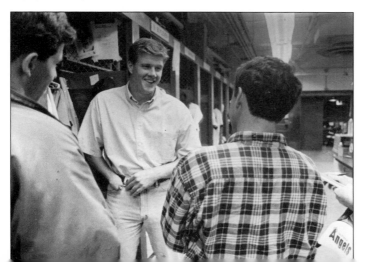

Abbott talks with reporters in the Angels locker room in April 1992. Abbott ended the 1991 season with an 18-11 record, and he and closer Bryan Harvey were voted the Angels' most valuable players by their teammates.

Mark Langston, and Chuck Finley, who were avid surfers. After one bodysurfing experience, when a wave pulled off his swimsuit, Abbott stuck to joking with the others about their surfing activities from the sand. With right-hander Kirk McCaskill, who had played hockey in Canada, and a few other Angels players, Abbott skated with the Los Angeles Kings of the National Hockey League in their off-season practice. He enjoyed cycling, working out, and reading. His taste in books ranged from *Summing Up* by Somerset Maugham to *Zen and the Art of Motorcycle Maintenance: An Inquiry into Values* by Robert Pirsig.

Abbott relaxed by listening to music; his favorite musicians include Don Henley, Neil Young, Roger Waters, Frank Sinatra, and Billie Holiday. One night, during the season, Abbott was in a hotel lobby in Baltimore with some players and reporters when a pianist began playing. He commented that playing the piano has been one of his longtime ambitions.

Abbott found plenty of the foods he liked to eat in Southern California, such as Mexican and Chinese, chicken and seafood. He also found love in Newport Beach when he met Dana Douty at a Halloween party. An economics major and a basketball player at the University of California, Irvine, Douty began dating Abbott. The two were married on December 14, 1991. Many of Abbott's friends could not go to California for the wedding, so when the couple visited Abbott's family in Flint for Christmas, Abbott hosted a reception for all his friends and former coaches. He even introduced Dana to Angelo's, but she is a vegetarian and declined the invitation to sample a Coney Island or a cheeseburger.

Unlike the heavily industrialized southern half of the Lower Peninsula of Michigan, the northern half of the Lower Peninsula consists of forests and cool, clear rivers and lakes. Abbott owned a log cabin near Harbor Springs on Lake Michigan, where he could enjoy some privacy, fishing, chopping wood, and walking in the forest.

In a moment of relaxation, Abbott and his wife, Dana, pose before a setting sun. Dana was an economics major and a basketball player at the University of California, Irvine, when she met Jim, and they were married on December 14, 1991.

As much as he loved pitching, Abbott disliked the business side of baseball. His record had improved in every respect in 1991 from the year before, and he believed his performance entitled him to be paid on a par with pitchers who earned several million dollars and who had worse records. Abbott was a favorite of Angels owner Gene Autry, a former cowboy movie star, but Autry left the salary negotiations to his wife, Jackie. She and Abbott's agent, Scott Boras, wrangled all winter until March 1992, when she broke off the contract talks. *Los Angeles Times* sportswriter Helene Elliott said, "It was the first time I ever saw Jim get mad. But he got over it quickly. He doesn't stay mad at anything." The two sides finally compromised at $1.8 million for one year.

Abbott felt comfortable and at home with the team for the first time during spring training, 1992. It was fortunate for the Angels that Abbott was in top physical condition because both Chuck Finley and Mark Langston were hobbled by minor injuries all spring. In his second start, against a loaded Texas team that had scored 53 runs in their first seven games, Abbott teamed with Bryan Harvey on a six-hit shutout. At Kansas City, he pitched five perfect innings before a rain delay prevented him from continuing. After three starts, he was 1-1 with an 0.89 ERA.

From then on, it was downhill all the way, literally in one case. On May 21, the Angels chartered a few buses for the 200-mile ride from New York to Baltimore. They were rolling along on the New Jersey Turnpike when the driver of the first bus lost control. The bus veered off the road, smashed through some small trees, fell over an embankment, crunched between two large trees, and tipped halfway over on its side. The trees held it from dropping into a deep ravine. Manager Buck Rodgers, seated in the traditional manager's place in the first seat by the door of the bus, suffered a fractured elbow and was out of action for several months. Abbott and the other pitchers riding in the second bus were unharmed. The scene must have reminded Abbott of the accident back in Ann Arbor he had survived with his high school friends when their car had overturned.

On the field, Abbott went a full month without a win. He had six losses in eight starts despite a 2.75 ERA. "I'm not happy with the way things have transpired," he said. "I had a lot of aspirations for this season and it's tough to see a lot of them go by the wayside."

Lance Parrish observed, "For some bizarre reason all the goofy things [errors and mistakes] that are happening happen when he's pitching." Parrish's comment prompted interim manager John Wathan to joke, "We've got to keep all the guns and sharp knives away from Abbie right now."

By July, Abbott was in the top 10 in innings pitched, complete games, shutouts, and earned run average, but he had only 4 wins against 10 losses to show for it. When there was speculation that he might be picked for the All-Star Game, he commented wryly, "I don't deserve to go. There's a lot of guys who have pitched better. Well, I don't know if they've pitched better, but they have the record."

His name came up in trade rumors—Toronto offered five players for him—but the Angels vowed they would not trade him unless they were convinced they could not sign him to a long-term contract. Negotiations had sputtered off and on during the season; Abbott wanted to stay in California, but he wanted to be paid what he thought was a fair salary.

He stayed in top condition by working the machines in the weight room, lifting weights, and bench pressing by resting one end of the weights on his forearm. Abbott, however, fared no better on the field for all of that, as Angels bats continued to go into a swoon every time he pitched. They scored two or fewer runs in 19 of his 28 starts. He pitched seven complete games but won only one. His 2.77 ERA was the fifth best in the league, but he finished with only 7 wins and 15 losses. As a fielder, he did not make a single error.

Long-term contract talks dragged into September; the Angels offered Abbott a four-year deal, which he called "a good faith offer [and] an honest effort to keep me with the Angels, and I'd like to be here."

It therefore came as a surprise to many observers when the Angels offered Abbott $16 million for four years, more than any player with just four years of experience had ever earned, and Abbott's agent turned it down, asking instead for $19 million. The Angels had meant to show their respect for Abbott by making their best offer at the start to avoid haggling with him, but it did not work.

The Abbotts wished to remain in California; Jim was settled there, and Dana's family lived nearby. Angels manager Buck Rodgers was one of many who believed that it was Abbott's agent who prevented him from accepting the offer, but Abbott denied it.

Rodgers called Abbott into his office and said, "Jim, you're 24 years old. With $16 million you can take care of your family for the rest of your life. And then if you want to shoot for the moon, in four years you're 28 and you can do the whole thing again."

Abbott's father could not understand his son's holding out for another $3 million, when he could never spend the money they were willing to pay him. "It is a matter of respect," Abbott told his father. "That's more important than the money. It is a way to measure how you are valued against your peers. That's what it is all about." One thing Mike Abbott was certain about, however: no amount of money would change his son.

Later, Abbott told writer Dave Cunningham that he had been on the verge of signing because he did prefer to stay in California. But the thought nagged at him that the Angels were not making a commitment to go all out to field a winning team. They had let pitcher Kirk McCaskill and first baseman Wally Joyner go to other teams. According to Abbott, the last straw occurred when the Angels left ace closer Bryan Harvey open to the expansion draft, and the Florida Marlins took him. "That hurt him pretty deeply," Cunningham said, "and it made him change his mind."

"When I was drafted by the Marlins," Harvey said, "that freed up some money, and the Angels should have done whatever it took to sign Jim. A player like that comes along maybe once in a hundred years, and what he meant to the players who looked up to him was invaluable to the team."

Unable to reach an agreement with Abbott, the Angels traded him to the New York Yankees on December 9, 1992, for minor leaguers J. T. Snow, Russ Springer, and Jerry Nielsen. Abbott had learned of the trade the night before from his mother-in-law, after he and Dana had returned from a vacation in Hawaii. He was shocked by the news. It meant they would have to find a new place to live for the summer, adjusting to new teammates, new friends, and an environment very different from southern California.

Criticism of the trade by outraged Angels fans came swiftly and fiercely. One newspaper received 600 calls in protest, but the public outcry did not alter the trade.

Yankees manager Buck Showalter and captain Don Mattingly called Abbott, pumping him up with the prospect of playing for a team with a chance to win the division

On January 7, 1993, during a visit to Yankee Stadium, Abbott ponders playing ball at the legendary ballpark. Abbott was unhappy about failing to negotiate a long-term contract with the Angels, but he later told a reporter, "Baseball is what makes me happy. . . . It's where my confidence lies. The pursuit of doing well in baseball is what I'm all about. Not contracts."

title. "There's an excitement at Yankee Stadium that's different from Anaheim," Showalter told him. "You'll like the New York fans. They stay for the whole game and hang on every pitch. They know baseball. They'll cheer you when you do well and boo you when you don't."

In January, Abbott went to New York for a press conference. The Yankees made it clear that they looked to him to be their ace, the one who takes the mound every fifth day and almost guarantees a win. "I respect the people in this league who do that," Abbott said. "Yes, I would like to be among those people."

For many ballplayers, playing for a New York team can seem like being slow-roasted on a spit; many free agents have accepted less money to play in cities where the media spotlight is not as harsh. Abbott, however, had no choice. He would not become a free agent until after the 1994 season. And before he ever threw a pitch for the Yankees, he felt as if he had been burned.

Third baseman Wade Boggs congratulates Abbott moments after he pitched a no-hitter for the Yankees. In the September 4, 1993, game against the Cleveland Indians, Abbott walked five and had one strikeout in his first major league no-hitter.

8

NEW IN NEW YORK

WHEN A PLAYER GOES TO ARBITRATION, it means he has decided what
salary he wants, and the team has made a lower offer. The Yankees
offered Jim Abbott $2.35 million for 1993; Abbott asked for $3.5
million. The two sides, with their lawyers and agents doing the talking,
met with an arbitrator, who listened to the arguments of each side and
chose the winner. There was no compromise.

Abbott's agent, Scott Boras, considered abrasive and antagonistic
by many baseball officials, made his pitch. He emphasized Abbott's
2.77 earned run average, fifth lowest in the American League in 1992.

The Yankees' lawyer, Jay Bergen, tore into Abbott. It upset and
angered Abbott to hear the criticism and negative comments being said
about him. "When you go in to represent the club," the lawyer explained later, "you have to point out the weaknesses the players have."

He harped on Abbott's 7-15 record of 1992 and his lifetime record of 47 wins and 52 losses.

Boras countered with the fact that the Angels had averaged only 2.55 runs a game for him, the lowest support for any starter in the majors that year.

As the arbitration hearing went on, Abbott fidgeted and grew hotter. He wondered why the Yankees had traded for him if they thought so little of him. He became even more infuriated when the arbitrator ruled against him.

Still hurting from the arbitration experience, Abbott reported for spring training in Fort Lauderdale, Florida, on February 18, 1993, likening the hearing to "the last chapter of a bad book. To the arbitrator and everyone else, it's just numbers," Abbott told reporters. "But to the player it's your sweat, your blood, your tears. So you take it personally. It's not easy coming to a new team and having that be your first association."

But Abbott recognized it as part of the business and determined to put it behind him. His salary was still "more money than I ever dreamed of making."

He looked sharp and impressive in exhibition games. After 19 innings he had not been scored on. Against the Florida Marlins on March 28, he had a chance to swing a bat, with no designated hitter allowed in the National Leaguers' park. Abbott was 1 for 4 and scored a run while hurling seven shutout innings for his second spring win.

Still close to his high school buddies, Abbott and his wife, Dana, stayed with Mark Conover when the Yankees played in Cocoa, Florida, where Conover is a teacher of special education.

After losing his first start in Cleveland, 4 to 2, Abbott pitched the Yankees' home opener on April 12. A sellout crowd of 56,704, including his wife and parents, roared their welcome to the Big Apple when Abbott walked in from the bull pen after completing his warm-up. He felt fit and ready as he walked out to face the Kansas City Royals. "There was something about New York, about wearing the uniform, about the fans and this team," he said later. "There was a play-off type atmosphere. It makes it a lot of fun."

It took Abbott just 83 pitches to complete a 4–1 victory. Pumped up for every pitch, he stood on the mound after the last out, arms raised toward the clear, crisp sky in a silent hurrah. He did not walk a batter. But, ever the perfectionist, he had stalked into the dugout after giving up a run in the sixth inning, angrily muttering to himself. "He doesn't feel like he should ever give up a run," said Yankees manager Buck Showalter.

New York reporters are the largest, toughest media crowd in baseball. They surrounded Abbott for more than 30 minutes, peppering him with questions, but for this day, at least, there was nothing except praise and warmth radiating from them. "This was a thrill," Abbott told them. "It's special."

Although he was wearing the celebrated Yankee pinstripes, Abbott soon began to feel as if he was back with the Angels replaying the 1992 season. The home opener was his only win in his first six starts, as the Yankees scored just 13 runs total for him; he was 1 and 5. "As a starting pitcher, your goal is to keep your team in the game," he said. "I did that, and if you do it enough, things should work out. I believe they will."

Not all the losses, however, could be blamed on lack of hitting. Five days after his brilliant debut at home, the Yankees could have scored eight runs and still lost. Abbott was wild and took a 9–0 pasting by Texas.

Another of the losses came on his first return to Anaheim, where he still felt at home. After New York tied the game at 2 to 2 in the top of the ninth, Abbott gave up a leadoff game-winning home run to Tim Salmon in the last of the ninth. While the other Yankees trotted off the field, Abbott, who had forgotten that he was no longer with the home team, waited for the umpire to throw him a new ball. "I guess I'm used to being on the home field," he said.

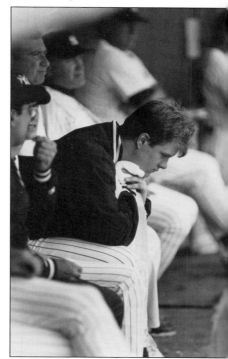

On August 18, 1993, Abbott looks discouraged as he sits in the Yankee dugout during a game against the Texas Rangers. He gave up seven hits and struck out two for his ninth loss of the season.

Nor could Abbott blame silent bats for his troubles in his first start in Detroit. On May 8, a Saturday afternoon, before his parents and many friends from Flint, the Yankees staked him to a 6–0 lead in the first inning. Unfamiliar with such prosperity, Abbott walked six, gave up six hits and seven runs in the first three innings, and got nobody out before he was lifted in the fourth. He later admitted to Detroit writers that it was the worst performance of his career, although the Yankees eventually won it, 10 to 8.

The season resembled a frustrating elevator ride, up and down with no stops. On May 3, trailing the Oakland A's 2 to 1 in the seventh, he came into the dugout, sat, and banged his right elbow against the back of the dugout in frustration, done for the day.

On May 24, after two strong outings, he was shelled for 12 hits by the Baltimore Orioles and driven to cover in a six-run fifth, but escaped with no decision. Five days later, he took a no-hitter into the eighth against the Chicago White Sox before giving up two hits in an 8–2 win. His cut fastball, breaking in to right-handed batters, produced 12 groundouts.

"Abbott has struggled with his location," sportswriter Jack Curry reported on May 29 in the *New York Times*. "He cracked 90 MPH just once in his last outing. . . . Whispers his velocity had disappeared and questions about his arm strength were certain to follow, but he was humming on Saturday."

On June 4, he was going for his fourth straight win when he gave up a base hit in the seventh that led to a 5–3 Rangers win. By now the press was giving Abbott a harder time than he had endured in Anaheim. They pointed out his tendency to give up decisive runs in the late innings, not the mark of a pitcher determined to excel as the ace of a staff. After a short-lived disaster in Cleveland, he left the ballpark and jogged for miles through the city, returning to find that the Yankees had pulled out a win. "There are some things you can't control in this game once the ball leaves your hands," Abbott said. "Baseball is a tough sport. It makes you pay in various ways."

He was strong-willed enough to take the criticisms with the praise. But he was as troubled by his performance as anybody and spent many a sleepless night talking to his wife about it. Twice Abbott went more than a month without winning.

Meanwhile, Abbott never drew back from his commitment to others. He held his annual clinic for the Challenger Division of Little League, which gives mentally and physically disabled children a chance to play baseball. On a field in Harlem in New York City, he played with them and talked about how he had reached his goals despite the lack of one hand. "Handicaps are all in your mind," he told them. "You put limitations in your mind on what you can do. . . . Don't let anything stop you from trying."

Abbott considered himself just another ballplayer. In the clubhouse, the only concession he made was to have his game jersey buttoned before it was hung in his locker so he could pull it on over his head. Nevertheless, he realized that some people see him as an inspiration to young people to try harder by seeing what he, himself, had accomplished. He received a constant stream of letters from youngsters with similar physical situations, or from their parents. In his answers, he told them, "Just because other people think you are handicapped, that does not make it so." To parents, he suggested, "Don't be discouraging. Always be encouraging and helpful. If people had told me I couldn't do what I did, I would never have tried."

Jim and Dana Abbott enjoyed life in New York. They rented an apartment on East 89th Street, in an area noted for its museums, shops, and restaurants. They walked a lot, appreciated the sights of the city, and did without a car for the first time in years. Abbott often rode the subway to Yankee Stadium, but usually took a taxi home at night.

Throughout most of June and July, the Yankees remained three or four games behind the AL East leaders. On the morning of July 22, there was only a one-game difference in the standings among the top four teams: Toronto, New York, Baltimore, and Detroit. By mid-August, the Yankees and Toronto were tied for first. The Yankees would spend a record 18 days tied for first without ever knocking the Blue Jays off their shared perch.

By virtue of hard work, Abbott had pulled his record up to 9 and 9. But every time he lost a game, the New York media sharks took another bite. Having trumpeted Abbott as the Cy Young Award winner before the season started, they had climbed out on a precarious limb. Now, no matter how well he pitched, he was not living up to their expectations. So they pounced.

"The New York media does an overkill," admitted Yankee broadcaster Tony Kubek. "We all do it. The city is full of itself sometimes. Most of the time Abbott has not been as bad as the New York media portrayed him to be."

Pitching coach Tony Cloninger felt stung by the media's criticism of Abbott. "It tore me up when people talked about his inconsistency. Every pitcher has 4 or 5 games a year where he gets hit hard, but a lot of times he gave up 4 or 5 runs on bloop hits and bleeders through the infield. In a few starts they scored 7 or 8 runs off him, and that caused his earned run average to be where it is [4.37]."

Pitching every fifth day, Abbott never varied his work routine. Cloninger, a 20-game winner with the Milwaukee Braves in 1965, commented on Abbott's methodology:

> He prepares for a ball game mentally and physically better than any pitcher I've ever been associated with After each game he pitches he goes over every hitter he faced and every pitch he threw. He keeps a log on every game he's pitched. We try to build off the positives each time.
>
> After a start he has a day off, then a work day, when we decide what we're going to work on and go out to the bull

pen. It may be locating on the outside of the plate, or a slow curve, or a change-up. He runs sprints and jogs, lifts weights, takes extra fielding practice; we hit comebackers at him in the outfield before games.

It's exciting for me to go to the bull pen on his work day and see how hard he works on things to prepare himself for the next start. Sometimes I think he's too hard on himself.

Abbott has some superstitions about his pitching. On days he pitches, he wears a special, "lucky" pair of jeans, a habit he clings to even when they seem to have holes in their lucky pockets.

Still hopeful that the highlight of his season would be a World Series start, Abbott arrived at Yankee Stadium on the rainy morning of Saturday, September 4, to pitch against the Cleveland Indians. He had won only one of his last six starts, but the Yankees were still just a game behind the Blue Jays.

Abbott's game plan this time included working the outside more and throwing more breaking pitches. All year, coach Cloninger and he had worked on his biggest problem: perfecting an effective pitch on the outside of the plate to right-handed batters. His arm movement automatically caused every pitch to cut in on righties, and after seeing him for four years, batters were adjusting by backing off the plate, knowing how the fastball would move. Some switch hitters preferred to bat left-handed against him, with marked success, to avoid being jammed by his cut fastball. "There is a fine line on that outside corner," Cloninger taught him. "If you pitch far enough outside and it cuts back over the corner, it's a great pitch. But if you throw to the corner and it cuts toward the middle of the plate, that's trouble."

Although he missed often enough to walk five batters, Abbott kept the Indians' hitters grounding out more than anything else. He took a 4–0 lead into the seventh without giving up a hit. He was fully aware of the situation; he had come close to a no-hitter before, on May 29, against the White Sox, and every pitcher knows exactly where things stand in a game at all times.

In the dugout, the players were unusually quiet; nobody spoke to Abbott when the Yankees were off the field. Manager Buck Showalter stirred uneasily on the bench. "I had to go to the bathroom for the last four innings," he said later, "but I was afraid to go. No one wants to be blamed for doing anything to jinx a no-hitter."

Third baseman Wade Boggs made a diving stop of a hard grounder in the seventh to keep the hitless streak alive. Standing at first base, Don Mattingly felt goose bumps forming on his arms as each of the Indians' hitters went down. "The hair on the back of my neck was standing up," he said later. "I think because it was Jim I felt a little something extra."

Cleveland Indian Carlos Baerga hits a grounder to Yankee shortstop Randy Velarde to secure the September 4 no-hitter for Abbott. The game was the high point of Abbott's first year with the Yankees, a year that found the left-hander struggling with an 11-14 record.

When Carlos Baerga grounded out to end the game, Abbott threw his arms high in the air and let out a loud but uncertain whoop. "I didn't know whether to be extremely confident or extremely thankful," he told the crowd of reporters after the game. "I'm just thrilled to death."

On the way to the dugout after the last out, Abbott waved to the crowd. As the cheers continued, he grabbed catcher Matt Nokes by the shirt and pulled him out onto the field for a hug and a bow. "He deserved to be out there as much as I did," Abbott explained.

Back in Flint, where Michigan football takes precedence over everything on autumn Saturday afternoons, Mike and Kathy Abbott learned about their son's no-hitter when the football announcers flashed the news.

That evening, Jim and Dana Abbott celebrated with Don Mattingly at one of their favorite neighborhood restaurants. But the excitement carried over to the next day. Abbott was used to being the center of attention, but for the first time since his rookie days with the Angels, the focus was on something he did, not on something he lacked.

When Abbott left his apartment on Sunday morning, September 5, photographers awaited him in the lobby. At Yankee Stadium, he found stacks of telegrams in his locker, many from disabled children who considered him a friend. "I never expected this to happen," he told the horde of reporters. "The fact that it happened in a pennant race makes it even better."

The grounds crew had dug up the pitching rubber and presented it, signed by all his teammates, to Abbott. The Hall of Fame requested his cap and the ball on which the last out was made. Mark Langston of the Angels had a bottle of champagne delivered to the Yankee clubhouse, and former Yankee pitcher Dave Righetti called him to impress on him the special significance of throwing a no-hitter for the Yankees, as Righetti, himself, had done 10 years earlier.

But Jim Abbott had thrown this one for more than just the Yankees. Albert Cortez, a 37-year-old who had been totally paralyzed in a car accident seven years before, sat in the third-base stands at Sunday's game and reflected, "A guy like Jim Abbott means a lot to a guy like me."

The no-hitter lifted the Yankees back into a tie for the lead with Toronto, but in many ways Jim's personal highlight coincided with the team's peak for the year. Any inspirational benefits it may have had on the team dissipated like windblown smoke. Two days later, they began a nine-day road trip to Texas, Kansas City, Milwaukee, and then into oblivion. Their starting pitchers won only one of the nine games. When they returned home, they were in third place, three games out, and sinking fast.

On Monday, September 13, club owner George Steinbrenner flew to Milwaukee and publicly blasted the players. He made clear his disappointment with Abbott and a few others, questioned some players' courage, and challenged them to be "good enough" to win.

"If he singled me out as being disappointing this year," Abbott said, "nobody likes to hear that. But he owns the team and is entitled to his opinion."

Recognized for his mental toughness, Abbott was also very sensitive. He claimed he gave the owner's remarks no further thought, but two days later, he made his worst start of the year. With two out in the first, he gave up a double, then walked three straight batters. The second inning was even uglier: four runs, four hits, two walks, and an early shower, the second quickest exit of his career.

In the weeks following his momentous no-hitter, Abbott gave up 14 runs and 25 hits in $15\frac{1}{3}$ innings. His record fell to 10 and 13. The Yankees headed to Toronto for a do-or-die series in late September, and died. But Abbott, always looking for the positives to build on, turned in a hopeful 7–3 win in the last game of the series.

"He was locating on the outside of the plate," Cloninger said, "offsetting his cut fastball moving inside, which we had been working on all season. He also threw some straight change-ups in that game and got some hitters out with it. I think he has a grip on that now and it will be a big pitch for him in the future."

For Abbott, the 1993 season ended as it began, with a score of 4 to 1; however, the Yankees lost this game. The loss left Abbott with 11 wins and 14 losses for the season.

"I don't think he had the kind of season he hoped to have," Jack Curry said. "And he became more guarded in the things he would say to us reporters. In the beginning he would talk more about his pitching and what might be going wrong, but at the end he was saying, 'I don't really want to get into that.'. . . After his win in Toronto we asked him about recapping his season. He wasn't real thrilled about trying to do that. He said, 'The past is the past. I'm not going to worry about it. It was not the season I thought it would have been, but it wasn't a total failure.'"

Cloninger believed that Abbott would be a successful pitcher for many years. "He's only 26 and still learning.

Yankee catcher Matt Nokes (No. 38) and third baseman Wade Boggs (center) congratulate Abbott after his no-hitter against Cleveland. Near the end of the season, Abbott told a New York Times *reporter, "It hasn't been the year I hoped it would have been. . . . I feel like I've given everything I had. If there has been fault, it's been in trying too hard. I can make it into a positive if I learned from the things I did wrong."*

He has the mental toughness required to pitch in New York, and the mental aptitude to adapt to any situation and overcome it with his work habits."

Abbott told sportscaster Tony Kubek, "I learned a lot from the success I've had this year. I'll take that with me this winter and regroup and improve on all those things."

Barring a trade, Abbott will remain with the Yankees at least through 1994, when he will be eligible for free agency.

Although he long ago dispelled any doubts about his fielding ability, Abbott's lack of a right hand presented an additional challenge. His search for another pitch—a split-finger fastball, the vogue pitch of the 1990s, or a circle change—was hampered by the fact that he could not conceal the ball in his glove as other pitchers do. "He cannot hide the grip he has on the ball," Kubek explained. "If he changes his grip before throwing, it could be spotted by a coach or the hitter or a baserunner, thus tipping them off as to what type of pitch was coming. But he is finding ways to disguise those things and come up with another pitch. Knowing Jim, he'll do it."

Near the end of the season, Buck Showalter called Abbott into his office. He had had many talks with the young left-hander during the year. "I wanted him to know I was very proud of the way he handled everything this year, how important he has been to us, and what we hoped to do down the road," Showalter explained. "It's a big adjustment coming from Anaheim to New York and people having such high expectations of him. But all you can do is what you are capable of doing, regardless of other people's expectations. . . . With a few breaks he could have had 16 or 17 wins, but he doesn't cry about it. He puts yesterday's successes or failures behind him and goes about his business."

Don Mattingly agreed. "A lot of players struggle their first year in New York. It's a tough place to come into and play. There were high expectations for Abbie when he came here, and New York is a 'do something for me, show me right now' kind of town."

With all his achievements, the one that Abbott's mother is most proud of is that "he is a compassionate, kind person who cares about others."

Nowhere was that better illustrated than one day in September after he had a terrible outing. "He got to the ballpark and it was pouring rain," Jack Curry recalled. "There was a bunch of kids standing around trying to get an autograph and there was Abbott, in the rain, no hat or umbrella or anything, signing for every kid."

"Jim is a gamer," his father said. "A gamer moves it up a notch when the game is on the line. A gamer wants the ball or a hitter wants the bat when it is do or die time. Jim has always been a gamer, in high school, college, the Olympics. If his team ever gets into a play-off or World Series, he will be the one who wants the ball for the deciding game 7."

Among players, managers, and reporters, the words most often used to describe Jim Abbott are "grace" and "class." Most players cringe at being labeled role models, and Abbott is no exception. But he cannot escape it if others choose to see him that way. "He is everything you would want a major league player to be," said Dave Cunningham of the Riverside, California, press. "Success will not change him. On the day he's inducted into the Hall of Fame, he'll be the same guy that he is today, the kind I would like my 9-year-old son to look up to and idolize. He's probably my favorite player of all I've met."

Sportswriter Helene Elliott covered the Angels for the *Los Angeles Times* when Abbott pitched there. At a symposium, she was asked, "Who would you list as your heroes?" She mentioned her father, then said, "No professional athletes. Seeing them up close and personal, most of the time we don't consider these guys heroes." She paused, then added, "Except Jim Abbott."

FURTHER READING

Johnson, Rick. *Jim Abbott.* New York: Macmillan, 1991.

Gutman, Bill. *Baseball's Hot New Stars.* New York: Pocket Books, 1989.

―――. *Jim Abbott.* Brookfield, CT: Millbrook Press, 1992.

Rolfe, John. *Jim Abbott.* New York: Sports Illustrated for Kids, 1991.

White, Ellen Emerson. *Jim Abbott: Against All Odds.* New York: Scholastic, 1990.

CHRONOLOGY

1967   Born James Anthony Abbott on September 19, in Southfield, Michigan; shortly thereafter the Abbotts move to Flint

1984   Gains first national recognition as starting quarterback in November for Flint Central High School

1985   Drafted by Toronto Blue Jays in June, but instead enrolls at the University of Michigan in Ann Arbor

1986   Pitches University of Michigan to first of two straight Big Ten championships

1987   Pitches for U.S. team in Pan-American Games; wins Golden Spikes Award as best amateur ballplayer

1988   Wins Sullivan Award as top amateur athlete; drafted by California Angels; pitches U.S. Olympic team to gold-medal win

1989   Makes major league pitching debut with the California Angels on April 8; records first major league victory, 3–2, over Baltimore, on April 24; ends the year with 12 wins, 12 losses, and a 3.92 ERA

1990   Ends the season with 10 wins, 14 losses, and a 4.51 ERA

1991   Wins 18 games for the Angels and loses 11, but has a 2.89 ERA; marries Dana Douty on December 14

1992   Ends Angels career with 7 wins and 15 losses; is traded to the New York Yankees on December 9

1993   Goes to arbitration and settles on $2.35 million for his first year with the Yankees; pitches the Yankees' home opener on April 12 and is victorious over the Kansas City Royals, 4–1; struggles throughout the season and works with pitching coach Tony Cloninger to improve his change-ups and throwing the ball on the outside of the plate; pitches a no-hitter on September 4 against the Cleveland Indians, lifting the Yankees back into a tie for the AL East lead with Toronto; Yankees do not make the play-offs and Abbott ends the season with a record of 11 wins and 14 losses

INDEX

Abbott, Chad (brother), 13, 20, 21, 57, 75
Abbott, Dana Douty (wife), 88, 91, 92, 96, 99, 103
Abbott, James Anthony (Jim)
  awards, 14, 45, 49, 50
  birth, 19
  childhood, 19–40
  college career, 14, 41–46, 50–51, 53, 57, 65, 75, 107
  contract dispute with Angels, 89, 91
  education, 23, 26, 38, 40, 41, 49, 50, 52
  football career, 30–32 33–36, 38
  handicap, 14, 15, 17, 19, 20, 21, 26, 27, 35, 36, 39, 41, 43, 47, 50, 53, 59–61, 63, 65, 67, 71, 72, 78, 79, 81, 84, 85, 87, 99, 106
  high school career, 27, 29, 32, 38–40, 53, 57, 65, 75, 107
  major league career, 13–17, 62–107
  marriage, 88
  meets Fidel Castro, 47
  at the 1988 Olympics, 14, 46, 49, 52–57, 62, 64, 107
  at the Pan-American Games, 46–49, 53, 73
  pitches no-hitter, 101–2, 103, 104
  as role model for physically challenged, 40, 45, 67, 77, 78, 99, 107

traded to New York Yankees, 92
Abbott, Kathy (mother), 13, 16, 17, 19, 20, 22, 26, 37, 41, 43, 49, 50, 57, 62, 69, 78, 96, 98, 103, 107
Abbott, Mike (father), 13, 16, 17, 19, 20, 21, 22, 24, 26, 27, 30, 37, 41, 44, 52, 57, 62, 69, 76, 78, 91, 92, 96, 98, 103, 107
Adams, Fran (grandmother), 57
Adams, Frank (grandfather), 13, 57
Angelo's, 37, 57, 74, 88
Ann Arbor, Michigan, 33, 41, 43, 81, 90
Archer, Jimmy, 60
Autry, Gene, 16, 89
Autry, Jackie, 89

Banks, Ernie, 75
Benes, Andy, 52, 55
Big Ten Conference, 33, 44, 45, 50, 51
Blanchard, Jeff, 26
Blyleven, Bert, 79, 80
Boras, Scott, 89, 95
Brock, Lou, 75
Brown, Mordecai "Three-Fingered," 59, 60

California, 13, 69, 88, 91, 92
California Angels, 15, 16, 51, 52, 62, 63, 65, 66, 67, 69, 70, 71, 72, 73, 74, 75, 76, 77, 79, 80, 81, 84, 85, 86, 87, 89, 90, 91, 92, 96, 97, 103, 107

Canseco, José, 66
Carlton, Steve, 72
Castro, Fidel, 47
Central High School, 27, 29, 30, 32, 34, 35, 36, 38, 40
Clark, Will, 49
Clemens, Roger, 80, 81
Cloninger, Tony, 100, 101, 104, 105
Connie Mack League, 32, 38, 57
Conover, Mark, 21, 30, 34, 96
Cortez, Albert, 103
Cross, Irv, 36
Cuba, 46, 47, 53, 55
Cuban national baseball team, 46, 47, 49

Daily, Hugh, 14, 59
Daley, Leavitt "Buddy," 60
Davis, Chili, 63
Detroit Tigers, 23, 24, 38, 40, 64, 74, 80, 97, 100
Donahue, Phil, 39, 43

Eufinger, Joe, 30, 31, 35, 36, 37

Finley, Chuck, 71, 87, 88, 89
Flint, Michigan, 13, 15, 20, 23, 24, 26, 30, 37, 39, 40, 53, 57, 69, 74, 81, 83, 87, 88, 98, 103
Flint Grossi, 32
Flint Journal, 26, 40, 62
Fraser, Ron, 46

Gooden, Dwight "Doc," 40
Grant Hamady Midget League, 26

PICTURE CREDITS

Courtesy Angelo's Coney Island, Flint, Michigan: p. 37; AP/Wide World Photos: pp. 12, 17, 25, 49, 58, 66, 67, 68, 70, 75, 77, 82, 87, 93; © 1993 Paul J. Bereswill/*Newsday*: p. 102; Courtesy California Angels: pp. 14, 63, 65 (Photo by V. J. Lovero), 89 (Photo by V. J. Lovero); Courtesy City of Mesa, Arizona: p. 64; Courtesy Flint Central Community High School: p. 30; *Flint Journal* Photo, Flint, Michigan: pp. 18, 23, 27, 31, 32, 33, 39, 74; Library of Congress: p. 60; National Baseball Library, Cooperstown, New York: pp. 61; Private Collection: p. 79; Reuters/Bettmann: pp. 2, 28, 48, 54, 94, 105; © 1993 Audrey Tiernan/*Newsday*: p. 97; UPI/Bettmann: pp. 22, 24, 42, 50, 56, 62, 76.

Norman L. Macht is the author of more than a dozen books for Chelsea House Publishers. His work also appears regularly in *Baseball Digest, Beckett's,* and *USA Today Baseball Weekly.* Macht is the coauthor with Dick Bartell of *Rowdy Richard,* and with Rex Barney of *Rex Barney's THANK Youuu for 50 Years in Baseball.* He is the president of Choptank Syndicate, Inc., and lives in Baltimore, Maryland.

ACKNOWLEDGMENTS
The author wishes to thank the following for their generous time and help: Mike Abbott; Mike Staisil; Mark Conover; Joe Eufinger; Dave Cunningham; *Long Beach Press-Telegram*; Tim Mead, California Angels media director; Dave Larzelere, *Flint Journal*; members of the Society for American Baseball Research; and the ballplayers who are quoted herein.

John Callahan is a nationally syndicated cartoonist and the author of an illustrated autobiography, *Don't Worry, He Won't Get Far on Foot.* He has also produced three cartoon collections: *Do Not Disturb Any Further, Digesting the Child Within,* and *Do What He Says! He's Crazy!!!* He has recently been the subject of feature articles in the *New York Times Magazine,* the *Los Angeles Times Magazine,* and the Cleveland *Plain Dealer,* and has been profiled on "60 Minutes." Callahan resides in Portland, Oregon.

Jerry Lewis is the National Chairman of the Muscular Dystrophy Association (MDA) and host of the MDA Labor Day Telethon. An internationally acclaimed comedian, Lewis began his entertainment career in New York and then performed in a comedy team with singer and actor Dean Martin from 1946 to 1956. Lewis has appeared in many films—including *The Delicate Delinquent, Rock a Bye Baby, The Bellboy, Cinderfella, The Nutty Professor, The Disorderly Orderly,* and *The King of Comedy*—and his comedy performances continue to delight audiences around the world.